WHEN IS STRONG – STRONG ENOUGH?

HOW TO PUSH THROUGH THE PAIN

By

Souraya Christine

Published by Write Touch Publishing

PUBLISHER'S NOTE:

Copyright © 2012 by Souraya Christine
Republished: 2014

All Rights Reserved, including the right of reproduction in whole or in part of any form.
ISBN-13:9780692026496
Library of Congress Catalog Card Number: in publication data.

When is Strong Strong Enough?
Written by: Souraya Christine
Edited by: David M. Good, Editing One
Text Formation: Write On Promotions
Cover Design and Layout: Donnie Ramsey
Printed in the United States of America

Dedication

This book is dedicated to my three beautiful children, especially the girls, Alyssa and Daija. I am not sure where I would be without you, but I am sure that God brought you into my life for a reason. This book will hopefully guide you through any turmoil that life may put into your path. Never allow anyone to take your strength or steal your joy. I pray that you never have to endure any of the pain that I have.

And for my son, Devin, I pray that you will always be respectful of women, and that you will use this book as a reminder of how imperative it is for you to maintain a strong and grounded relationship with God, and family.

I love you all more than the life that fills my body, and always will, no matter what.

Letter to my Mother

Dear Mommy,

I have looked at my entire life as having mostly been filled with pain. I will admit that, for much of the pain, I blamed you. I blamed you for not knowing, for not protecting me, for not seeking help for me, for not understanding me. All the while, not realizing that my story was being written for a much greater purpose. Also not realizing that you were my living angel and that you performed as a mother to the very best of your abilities. I credit you today, instead of resenting you, for creating a strong and independent woman; I love you today, instead of feeling contempt toward you, for never turning your back on me; most importantly though, I forgive you today, instead of harboring feelings of betrayal and hurt, for it is better for my soul to do so.

There were many nights I would lay awake in tears wondering why....why I was chosen to suffer, to not know my biological father, to be so overly independent, non-trusting, and so afraid that I rejected any man who tried to care for me. These were all things and more that I needed to release; things that God gave me peace about; things that He instructed me to forgive for, as I too would be forgiven for the things I have done, and the decisions that I have made bringing about my own pain.

I am writing you this letter so that you will understand that this book was not written to demean you in any way. I love you, you have been an inspiration, loving mother, and best friend throughout my life. I needed to do this in order to heal and help someone else who may be experiencing any of the things that I have experienced. The processes that I went through emotionally toward and about you were all a large part of my testimony. You will forever be the wind beneath my wings....and I shall forever honor you!

With a most intense love,

Souraya Christine

Acknowledgements

Before anyone else, I must thank my father...my heavenly father. Without you father, none of this would even be possible. I admit to going through long periods of despair, wondering why you allowed certain things to happen to me, but I realize now that you had a purpose for my life, and that all I had to do was endure. You gave me a testimony and the will and strength to use what I have been through to breathe life into someone else. And it is all for your glory!

To my mother...I thank you for having my back...always, even when I didn't necessarily accept it. I thank you from the bottom of my heart for doing your very best to have raised me and for participating so faithfully in the upbringing of my children. Nothing you do goes unappreciated. Thank you for being you!

To my incredibly amazing children Alyssa, Daija, and Devin...the three of you are my world. Everything I do, with God's grace, is for the betterment of our lives. I apologize to you for being a single parent and having to work so much to provide for you. I apologize for not hugging and kissing you as much as I should have. I apologize for putting men and other situations before you. I am truly grateful for your unconditional love and so very proud of the tremendous individuals that you are all becoming. Mommy loves you!

To my "day job", Sharon and Donna...I just wanted to express my sincere gratitude for putting up with me during this entire process. You ladies are amazing and I will forever be thankful to have known and worked alongside you.

To my dear friends Iveth Becker-Bethune and Cynthia Evans...words cannot describe how I feel about you two. God brought you into my life right when I needed you most, and for that I will forever be grateful. Your kindness, thoughtful words, helping hands, open hearts, and loving embraces helped me more than you could ever imagine throughout this journey. I love you ladies and pray that these friendships will endure the tests of time.

To my baby sister Brandi...although you and I have not always gotten along, I have spent my entire life trying to keep you protected from so many things. I don't know if I have always been successful, but just know that I have always loved you with my whole heart and always will... throughout eternity.

To Luther...Although you suffered from a gripping addiction throughout my life, I am eternally grateful and proud of the fact that you made the attempt to step up to the plate as my father. You guys had me fooled for quite some time, so I guess you were doing something right. I am thankful to you for loving my mother enough to be willing to raise me as your own, and for that alone, you will always be "dad".

To Bishop Clinton House, First Lady Mary House and the entire Mountaintop Faith Ministries Family...I don't even know where to start. When I stumbled upon your church, I was weak, heart-broken, losing hope, and headed fast down the wrong path...again. Your words, acceptance, and prayers quickly brought me back and made me realize just how very blessed I am. I feel forever indebted to you for saving my life. Had I gone to the church that I was intending to visit on that Sunday in August of 2011, I may not be where I am today. God knew exactly who and what I needed to create a detour smack in the middle of the desolate road I was on. I love you all with every fiber of my being and whether or not you ever know me personally, know that my life, my soul, my heart, and my mind have been mended since stepping through your doors.

Finally to everyone with whom I have had either the pleasure or displeasure of knowing throughout the course of my life...I thank you, wholeheartedly, for the role you played. The way you touched my life, negatively or positively, has helped to shape the person I am today. A woman! A woman who has been bent but not broken; cracked but not shattered; and scarred but still maintains the ability to keep my head high, smile, and press forward. I have been given a joy from God that no person or circumstance can take away...one that I have spent my entire life seeking in all the wrong places. I finally found this joy in Christ.

A special THANK YOU to my newfound church family, Nehemiah Ministries. Your love has captured my heart. Thank you for making me a part of your family, for supporting my dreams and for "Rebuilding Broken Walls in People's Lives". You ALL are simply amazing! Pastor Kelcey West and First Lady and Evangelist Carmen West, I do not even have words to describe my love for you. All that I can say is thank you.

INTRODUCTION

I decided to write this autobiography, not because I am anyone famous, or because I have lived some marvelous life. Nor am I seeking any level of sympathy from any person. Just the opposite is true. I am not famous at all, and my life can be described, by most accounts, as a living hell. For that reason, I am staying up well past my bedtime every night reliving the same horrible nightmares that plagued most of my early years. I am doing this with hopes that some young lady will be able to cope, in a positive way, with whatever traumatic situation she is faced with. If I can assist just one young lady in recognizing and channeling her strengths, then I will feel as if my goal, with writing this book, has been accomplished. This book begins in my early childhood years, and will briefly outline all of the horrible circumstances, that I could recall, that I endured, and how I managed to survive them. Most of the names have, of course, been changed to protect the subject's identities. Should anyone feel distressed by the writing of this book, please know that it was not my intention to cause you to feel this way. I simply believe that facing your true feelings is imperative for the healing and growth process.

On the following page, you will find an original poem that, very fittingly, will begin my life story. So sit back and relax, and perhaps grab a box of tissue. You probably will not enjoy what you are about to read, but I am confident that it will help you, at one point or another, in dealing with traumatic events.

Note to Self

Some days I feel I can't go on,

The pain, the grief, I feel so withdrawn.

Their eyes are burning through my soul,

Penetrating me as if they know.

Can they tell? Can they see what I've been
through?

Of course not, how could they? It was between
me and you.

My life was not displayed for them,

I wasn't put on trial for them to condemn.

Why do you care what they think of you?

"I don't" I thought, "You just think I do".

It is God that I am trying to please,

My secrets, my heart, I know He sees.

Truthfully though, I'm afraid of this,

For it is Heaven that I fear I'll miss.

WHEN IS STRONG – STRONG ENOUGH?

HOW TO PUSH THROUGH THE PAIN

TABLE OF CONTENTS

FOREWORD

I am Souraya's oldest daughter. We've shared much laughter, much pain, much joy, many tears, and many smiles. In a way, we kind of grew up together. Having a teen mom, I probably grew up much faster than I ever needed to and there were times I silently blamed her for this. When you're young you don't really see the sacrifices and pain someone goes through for you. You just scream for attention from the one person that's never supposed to let you down, not realizing that that person is craving the same attention.

I've gone through many things I shouldn't have, seen many things I shouldn't have, and made many decisions I shouldn't have. One thing I can say about this woman, my mom, if nothing else, is that she never took her love away. No matter how many fights we've had, no matter how many times we disagreed, no matter how many times I moved away to not have to deal with her or her not have to deal with me, she loved me. No matter how much wrong I did, no matter how much I hurt her, no matter how much she had to fight for me, she loved me. Growing older I've realized everything she's done for me and I know words will never allow me to show the gratitude I feel or thank her enough. She's made an infinite number of sacrifices for me, both big and small. Putting a halt to her own life, she left everything she knew and moved our family from Cleveland to Las Vegas.

I was headed down the wrong path, possibly even a remake of her history and she knew it. She did what needed to be done as a parent and got me out of that environment. I had to put her through more pain in moving to Las Vegas because for the first couple of years you would have thought I was the devil's child. You could take the girl out of Cleveland, but you couldn't take the Cleveland out of the girl. I did some things just to spite her. I was so bitter about her taking me away that I couldn't see then that in reality she saved me. She is my angel.

Growing up I took a lot after her without even realizing it. Her attitude was vicious and defensive with everyone and after suffering through failed relationship after failed relationship, her emotions were cold. Having grown up around this, my attitude mocked hers from the day I could talk. Every man that tried to care for me I didn't trust, I ignored, I was evil to, and I showed absolutely no emotion for. I would let no one get close to me emotionally to ensure (or so I thought) that no one had the power to break me. However, after realizing how much she was trying to help me not be like her I started to work on my attitude. I started to care a little more; I started to give a little more. She did this for me unconsciously. She is my rock. She is my strength. She is my light. She is the love in my heart.

I've seen her emerge from a bitter, angry, attitudinal being to a loving, kind, caring, faithful woman that only God could have created. I love her. As you explore these pages and relish in the depths of the ups and downs of the journey of her life, I pray that you find strength and healing.

I pray that you see that you are not alone in whatever struggle you are facing. I pray that you realize that God will not bring you to something that he will not bring you through. More than anything, I hope you see the strength he is bestowing upon you and realize that you are, indeed, STRONG ENOUGH!

Love,

Alyssa Cowsette

1st born of Souraya Christine

Stop Crying Chapter 1

"Oh my goodness...I am so tired", is all that's going through my head as I'm running down the street to my home, crying and screaming in fear. Why are these girls chasing me home every day? I mean, I'm only five years old. I'm quite sure I haven't done anything to them. Was it just because I looked weak? I was very scrawny; tall and lanky for my age, and a very pretty child if I might say so myself. Why would these twin girls possibly want to hurt me? Funny, I can remember their looks rather well. One was fat and one was skinny, light-skinned, long hair. Not very attractive though. I only, however, recall one of their names. For purposes of this recount, we'll call her Angelina, and her sister we'll call Evelyn.

These girls had it in for me. Every day, the chase was on. It had gotten to a point that I no longer wanted to go outside to play. Stepping outside would make me instantly nauseous. Pretty soon, the twins had enlisted the assistance of other girls on the street to torture me. I remember being surrounded by a fairly large circle of girls, shoving me back and forth, pulling my hair, and hitting me. I was terrified. I wasn't a fighter. I had absolutely no intentions of fighting, not even to defend myself. Where were the parents of these children? For that matter, where were my parents? I mean, we're right outside of our homes and no one recognizes this commotion? Do they assume that we're all just playing? This was ridiculous, and getting completely out of control.

"Stop crying", my mom would say. "You don't let anyone bully you. If you can't stand up and fight, then I'll beat your ass when you come in this house." Wow! I guess that's one way to build character. Or begin the cycle of insanity. So what choice did I have? It was either get beat up by these girls and my mom, or learn to fight back. One day, while walking home from school, I guess about age six by now, the chase began again. Were they not tired of harassing me yet? I suppose I was still an easy target. Today, however, I had a trick for everyone, unbeknownst to even me. Instead of running into the house, as I normally would, I ran into my backyard. The twins only followed me to the driveway however, where they stood, taunting me. I emerged from the backyard with a small tree. "What do you think you're going to do with that", one of them said, and before I realized it I was charging at them like a bull, screaming. One of the sisters ran off screaming, the other one however, the one that really thought she was tough, stayed to fight. All that I recall is my mom coming outside, into the driveway, attempting to pull me off of this girl, who now lay on the ground being pummeled by the tree I was wielding. I remember crying and laughing at the same time, and hollering at her, I'm sure with some obscenities because, in my youth, my mom cursed like a sailor. Eventually my mother was able to get me off of the girl - the skinny twin it was, Evelyn. Needless to say, that hell was over, and I never again had an enemy on that street. Well at least not one that would admit it.

Funny how much a person can actually deal with, especially when it's all at one time. During this same period in my life, another trauma was going on inside my home. I had two cousins, later to find out they weren't blood related, but we'll discuss that in more detail later. These two cousins, both female, would come to spend the night quite often. One of them, LaTrece, was my favorite at the time. The other cousin was a few years older than us. Her name was Tammy, someone whom I quickly began to dislike. Initially, things were good. We had so much fun together. LaTrece's mom would keep my hair braided, and I wouldn't be so worried about the bullying outside. However, at some point, Tammy decided that she wanted more from me. She would start by forcing me to touch her. First her breasts, then her vagina. I was very uncomfortable, and didn't really understand what was going on. Why did she want me to touch her private areas? Nonetheless, because I was obviously fearful of people, I did exactly what she told me to do. This would continue every time she visited my house, eventually progressing to more indecent acts. I recall, one day, the three of us were in the backyard picking fruit off the tree, and she pulled her pants down and told me to lick her vagina. I, of course, declined, however she became pretty forceful, and I eventually obliged. This was the first I had ever been introduced to this type of behavior. I had no clue what was going on, or if she would hurt me if I didn't comply with her requests. After all, she *was* from the projects, they were tougher, right?

Because of these traumatic events, I began misbehaving in school. Acting out, as they say. What other way did I have to deal with the issues at hand? I couldn't tell anyone about my cousin abusing me. No one would like me if I did. My family would think I was starting trouble, wouldn't they? This is what Tammy would tell me. I had only one outlet – misbehaving. Ok maybe two, because I began writing poetry around this time as well.

I've never revealed this situation to anyone before. Reliving it today as I write it is still a little disturbing. In fact, until now, I've never even faced this particular event. Thankfully, we soon moved and my parents weren't together much longer, so my contact with Tammy slowly and completely faded away. I'm not really sure how my family, upon reading this will even tolerate this divulgement. Oh well, it is an autobiography, designed to assist people with overcoming grief and pain. This was surely painful for me, and I am still on the road to recovery.

Push Through:

Tough love, as they call it, works in some cases, when you are attempting to break a cycle of behavior. For me, it was the cycle of being afraid of getting beat up. Unfortunately, threatening more violence may not have necessarily been the proper way to show tough love. Additionally, because so many other problems were unfolding at the same time, it didn't really work so well on me. I would say to parents of young children, try to learn and understand what your child is going through before you begin to try to attack or solve the problem. The problem you believe it to be may not be the true root cause, but instead the effect. Realizing and then facing your fears is a very difficult task for a young child. It's because their brains and thought processes are not yet fully developed; they can't fully comprehend their options when dealing with stress.

Unfortunately, at this young age, they generally just act. The things you experience start to build your character. Some of the paths we take in life are determined by some of the things we saw during this impressionable stage. We adapt to our environment. In hindsight, I would highly suggest being open and talking with your parents, guidance counselor, or a trusted school teacher about traumatic events you're experiencing. They are better equipped, mentally, to deal with the options, and the consequences. Trust me on this one.

The Theft of Innocence Chapter 2

I grew up in Cleveland, OH - East Cleveland, to be exact, and on the outside I was a normal 7 year old child; riding bikes, skating, and playing outside with my friends. I had quite a few fights, but of course everyone thought that to be normal kid stuff. On the inside however, I was being eaten alive! Figuratively speaking of course. I was suffering from one of the worst forms of abuse imaginable. The worst part – no one even had a clue, and would not for the next four years. My mom had been separated from my father, for a couple of years, because of a very strong drug addiction my father had, that had completely taken over his life. My mom now had a live-in boyfriend, "Howard". I must say, I am having a hard time concealing the identities of people who had absolutely no problem hurting me! Hmmmm...food for thought I suppose.

Howard was a firefighter for the city of Cleveland. He was *supposed* to be a role model for young children. Someone who protected people from harm, I thought. He, however, had a very dirty little secret. One that would ruin his career for sure. At least two or three times a week, as we all lay asleep, Howard would sneak into the room I shared with my then 3 year old sister, in the middle of the night. I thank God, even today, that he never touched my little sister, but I, unfortunately, was not so lucky. I remember being in a deep sleep, and would feel my panties slowly coming down until they reached my ankles, and then the floor. I would feel what I thought was the largest hand in the world cover my mouth, and a voice whisper in my ear, "If you scream, or ever tell anyone, I will kill you and your little sister." Then I would feel his penis slide between my thighs as I tried, with all my might, to keep them shut. I don't believe that he ever actually completely penetrated me; however, he came very close on many occasions. I believe, to this day, that the slight struggle I was able to put up took up too much time for him to ever be able to finish the job before someone woke up. Unfortunately, that didn't stop him from trying.

At this time, we lived in a two bedroom, two story townhouse. I recall, one night, my mom having a party downstairs, and I was upstairs taking a bath. My bedroom was right next to the bathroom. I came out of the bathroom, wrapped in a towel, about to get into my night clothes, when I was approached near my bedroom door. I was startled by Howard standing behind me. There was a jar of Vaseline on my dresser, and I recall him sticking his hand in the jar, pulling out his penis, and rubbing the Vaseline on himself, while trying to force me into rubbing it on his penis as well. He said to me, "this time it will work". He then proceeded to try and force himself into me again as I just stood there in shock. Lucky for me, since we were standing, it just wasn't working. Plus I could tell that he was nervous about someone coming upstairs, so back to the party he went. Funny, I don't even remember crying.

I recall a day my mom left me home with him. I was so scared to be alone with him, because then he could have his way without a care in the world. This day, I was sitting on the couch, looking at the television, when he stepped in front of me and tried with lots of force, to stick his penis in my mouth. "Come on," he said. "Your mom does it all the time, why can't you?" Hmmm....maybe because I'm like 8, and don't even know what is going on? "Do you think you're too good for this?" he asked. Well, he met his goal this time. He managed to get it into my mouth, and though now I wish I had bitten it, I was simply too afraid to move. I can still recall the taste.

I do not recall each individual instance over the next four years, but the finale – the final occurrence – I remember vividly. We had since moved up the street, into a two-family house. My mom had gone somewhere with my grandmother, and left me alone with Howard, who was obviously overjoyed at this fact. He forced me into the bedroom and onto the bed he shared with my mom. There was a pornographic movie playing in the VCR. He, very politely, asked me to please perform the same acts that the ladies were doing in the movie, while he, not so politely, stuck his fingers into my vagina. He tried again to force me to give him oral sex, while continuing to fondle me. By this time I was eleven years old, and a little bit wiser I suppose. One thing was for sure – I was completely fed up! For what seemed like forever after this nightmare had begun, I heard my mother and grandmother come through the door. I ran out into the living room crying, however still somewhat afraid to tell what was happening. My grandmother, God rest her soul, asked me directly if Howard had touched me in my private areas, and what a relief it was for me to say "YES!" and finally feel free. My mom immediately told him to leave the house, which to me, just wasn't enough. And so started the resentment toward my mom.

Now I remember loving my mother to death, even though I was with my grandmother quite often. There would be times when I would get a spanking, for whatever reason, and run to my grandmother's house. I always felt that she loved me more than my mother did, and I always felt safe with her, although her husband liked to hug me and have me sit on his lap – which made me feel very uncomfortable. He also drank way too much, which made it that much worse. I must say that as long as I was in her room, sitting next to her on the bed, or sleeping on a pallet on the floor by her bed, I felt that nothing could harm me. My grandmother was affectionately called "Bunny". She was my rock! She forced me to church practically every Sunday, where I learned about God and prayer. Although I hated it then, I must admit that the relationship I developed with God eventually carried me through this and many other situations.

Apparently God was keeping a watchful eye over Howard too because I saw him again many years later, walking down a residential street. As I made a U-turn to follow him, pulling my gun out from beneath my seat, he disappeared between some houses. I am sure that I would have killed him on this day, but I probably wouldn't be able to share my story with you today had I done that.

Over the first eleven years of my life, I had turned into a horribly mean and hateful person. I was engulfed in so much pain that it consumed me. The pain manifested into terrible anger and misbehavior. After all, I had been molested most of my life, bullied, lied to (which you'll read about next), and had developed an unmasking contempt for my own mother. It seemed as though I was in some form of trouble almost on a daily basis. If I wasn't sassing off to teachers in school, I was fighting, or simply giving attitude to anyone who crossed my path. I even remember taking a knife to elementary school one day for fear of a promised fight. The interesting part is that I was amazingly intelligent, and remained so throughout all of this. I was in all honors classes, at a "gifted" school, and was always speaking or performing in some play or event that the school was having. I also wrote a lot of poetry. Unfortunately, it has all since been lost, otherwise I would share some of it with you. I recall getting an invitation to be featured in Who's Who, for the work that I was doing and the grades that I was getting. I'm not sure what ever happened with that. I believe that staying busy with school functions and writing my poetry helped to ease and funnel some of the pain I was feeling. Through all of the pain I felt, and trouble I got into in elementary school, there were two amazing people that I will take this opportunity to thank. One of whom I'm sure is no longer alive, Mrs. Elisabeth Clarke, and the other is Mrs. Dianna England. Without these two amazing women, I don't think that I would have been able to cope with life – as it were.

Even though they had no idea what was happening to me at home, they both took me under their wings and tried to steer me in the right direction. I was constantly lashing out at the world, but bless their hearts, they never gave up on me. They encouraged me to pursue the lead speaking roles, and write and read my poetry in front of hundreds of people. They even made it possible for the one and only phenomenal woman herself, Maya Angelou, to come to a performance and meet me! That was the absolute best experience of my life, at the time. Mrs. England was my sixth grade teacher, and to this day, the person that I looked up to the most. She would always let me come stay the night at her house, and play with her dog, "Girlfriend". She was always behind me, coaching me, always insisting that I do better. I truly admired her for that. I wonder though, if she had known what was going on in my life, would she have treated me any differently? I suppose I'll never know the answer to that, but I am truly glad to have had her in my life.

There was also another strong figure in my early childhood – my grandfather. His name was Wilbur. His friends referred to him as "Doc", but my sister and I called him "Papa". And although my grandfather was involved in many things in the streets, none of which will be discussed here so as not to speak ill of the dead, he was still the most amazing man in the world to me. He was always smiling when he saw me, and that would light up my whole world. I believe he went to his grave not knowing whatever happened to me. I can assure you, had he known, "Howard" would only be a name on a tombstone. My Papa would always come around with pockets full of money! He would say to my sister and me, "If you can guess how much this is – you can have it." Of course we were never right, but he would always give us a few dollars anyway.

Papa had gotten very ill, with a variety of health problems, and had become bedridden and terminal. On his death bed - mind you I was only eleven years old, he decided to let me in on a "little" family secret. The man who I believed to have been my father all of these years, was not actually my father. What?! That's right; he was, in fact, my little sister's father, not mine. Wow! This was exactly what I needed in my life right now – more trauma. What a devastating blow this was. This caused even more resentment toward my mom. Why had she not told me the truth? Didn't I deserve to know who my real father was? Apparently not – and for the record, I still don't know. What a great way to start middle school...watching my grandfather take his last breath, testifying in court against my abuser – who by the way was arrested at the fire house on charges of molesting me, and learning the heartbreaking truth about my existence. I never once recall however, actually confronting my mother about this atrocity.

No one really liked me in school because I was just too mean and treated most people like dirt. I did have one friend however; we still call each other sisters to this day. Her name is Tamara. We started school together in elementary. Tamara and her family were my refuge. She, outside of Mrs. England and Mrs. Clarke, was the best thing that ever happened to me. We became really close in middle school, and I honestly don't know how we have remained so close over the years. She seemed to be so much more sophisticated than me. Well, however it happened, I sure am glad that it did! I don't think you could have pried us apart with pliers. She was always someone I could lean on, look up to, and trust. Trust was just not something that worked well for me. Funny to me now, I wouldn't have traded my self-made "big sis" for anything in the world, but would have given my God given little sister away willingly. My real sister, Brandi, and I never really got along. We fought like cats and dogs. In hindsight, I think a part of me blamed her for my being molested. The whole time I only thought of protecting her. I am sure that I could have easily moved to my grandmother's, or told Mrs. England what was happening to me, but then I would have risked him hurting my sister, and I simply could not have that. Perhaps it was also due, in part, to my finding out that we didn't share the same father. Who really knows? What I do know is that, today, I love my sister more than I could ever express in words, and pray that she knows that.

Push Through:

During my early school-age years, I was subjected to numerous traumas. I never understood how a God, who the Church claimed loved me so much, could allow such horrible things to happen to one of His children. I couldn't grasp how so many people, who were supposed to love me, couldn't see the pain that I was enduring and were so quick to just write me off as "bad". I blamed my mother for everything that happened to me, and held animosity against her for years. I had an attitude problem, and was mean and hateful because I was hurting. My heart and soul were aching, and no one ever knew. Everyone blamed me for my actions, when, to tell you the truth, it was the only way I knew. Once my mother and grandmother found out about the abuse, it was simply swept under the rug – so to speak. I never received any counseling or support of any kind, nor did we ever discuss it. I was just supposed to be strong.

Parents, be more in tuned to your child's behaviors. Question them and talk to them about things, even if you do not suspect any foul play. No matter what, show them that you are there for them, and that you would never knowingly allow anyone to harm them. Please continue to reassure them of that. If something traumatic does happen to them, make sure you support them and get them some counseling. Talking to someone who does not know your child, is non-judgmental, and is experienced in dealing with these situations, may be exactly what they need. You may not always know the best thing to do or say, but trust me when I tell you, they need whatever type of love you can show them. Allow your child the opportunity to vent their frustrations in a positive way. Encourage them to talk, draw, write or something. Most importantly, read between the lines. I am not suggesting that you be nosey or snoop around in their rooms, but be aware and listen very carefully, because they may be trying to tell you something without ever speaking a word.

Children and young adults, please pay attention: If you are going through or have gone through any of the things discussed here, please tell someone. I know you are afraid, perhaps even for your life, but believe me you may not be able to *live* your life holding on to such horrendous secrets. If there is a teacher, a counselor, a coach, a minister, or anyone that you trust in school or church, please tell them. Just close your eyes and let it all out. I assure you that the result will allow you the ability to take a deep breath and relax. Now, the person that harmed spent less than two years in jail, but I'd like to think that the justice system is a lot better now, and is processing these offenses more diligently and giving stricter sentences. Don't worry about how much time they will get, just know that you will finally be able to live your life, as a child, without having someone interfering with that. Know that they will have to answer for their crimes to a much higher authority one day, and that God will avenge your pain no matter how bad your faith may have been shaken.

Romans 12:19

"Dearly beloved, avenge not yourselves, but rather give place unto wrath: for it is written, Vengeance is mine; I will repay, saith the Lord."

The Teen Years Chapter 3

I was eleven when I first started middle school, and turned twelve that December. In between that time I met a guy who completely captured my heart. His brother, however, was the one who was actually into me. I just didn't like his brother like that. I had my sights set on "Drew" (or at least that's what we'll call him here). Drew was a bad boy. He had already been into the streets, so to speak, and was mostly interested in "getting" any girl he could. One day, he chose me. We started hanging out a lot. I would always come visit him on what we all called "the hill" and we would simply hang out. I vividly recall sitting on his lap and feeling how large his penis was underneath me. Now I knew that he wanted to have sex with me, this was his 'thing'. However, after going through all of the stuff I had been going through, I was terrified. I certainly couldn't allow him to be my true "first". Although I was extremely crazy about this boy, I never let him get past second base. The great thing was, for the most part, he remained respectful, and therefore we remained friends – and still are to this day. We were boyfriend and girlfriend for a little while in middle school, but since I wasn't putting out, that didn't last very long. I had learned to become emotionally detached so I wasn't really affected by the break up. I even went on to "date" other boys in middle school as well, some of whom were quite fond of me, although I was never really able to reciprocate those feelings.

Around this time, my mother met and became involved with a pretty big drug dealer - "Robert". Back then selling drugs seemed to be the thing to do. It seemed to be what we related with success. The problem with Robert was that his temper was out of control, as was the case for many men in his line of work. He didn't raise his voice too often at my sister or me; however I do recall my mom being victim to it... often. I believe that he raised his hand upon her more times than I am actually aware of, but I'll share with you the time I remember. We had since moved into yet another home, and truthfully, I was just hoping for better days. Ha! No such luck. I was around 12 or 13 years old at the time, hanging out in my bedroom. Suddenly I heard loud banging noises and screaming and crying coming from the bathroom. I ran in there and found my mom on the floor and Robert standing over her, shaking and hitting her, and yelling obscenities at her. Without thought, I ran into the kitchen and grabbed the biggest knife I could find, ran back into the bathroom, and tried with all of my might to thrust the blade into the back of his skull. I suppose he probably thanked God for the thickness of skulls that day, because the knife only pierced his skin. By this time I was terrified and ran down the back stairs to the neighbors and called the police. When they arrived, I let them in from downstairs and took them up the back stairs into our home. We found that the fight had progressed into the living room. There was blood everywhere! Some of it was from my mom, but most was from the hole in the back of his head. I remember the police making him leave the house, but I don't recall, and highly doubt, whether my mom ever pressed charges. What I do recall is that they ended up back together, and he ended up back in the house.

Now Robert was nice to me, and told everyone that I was his daughter. He affectionately referred to me as, "Boobie". Being a drug dealer afforded him the ability to buy nice things for us sometimes. However, from that earlier incident forward, I never felt as close to him. For years I felt as if he would somehow retaliate against me for stabbing him. I thought things were alright for a while, until one Sunday, as my grandmother dropped me off at home after leaving church, there was an ambulance in front of my house. My heart instantly sank, thinking that Robert had truly hurt my mom. As I ran up crying and screaming, "What did you do to my mother?" I felt nauseous watching the EMS roll my mom past me. To my surprise, and somewhat relief, I found out later that she had suffered a nervous breakdown, and although I'm sure he had a huge hand to play in that, he hadn't actually done anything to her at that point. I recall one relapse she had where I woke up to her vacuuming my bedroom floor in the middle of the night, crying. I'm not sure that she had any other episodes after that.

Once middle school had ended, I was thirteen, and it was on to high school! Catholic school no less. I turned fourteen in my ninth grade year. During this time I met another young man. His name was "T". I like to think that T was my first love. We were really into each other, and spent as many moments as possible together. Usually it was at the house he shared with his parents in Cleveland Heights. T was another bad boy – apparently I'm developing a pattern here. He was in a street gang, and fought all of the time. Heck, sometimes I even participated, or at least had his back when something happened.

Our relationship had developed to the point that you hardly ever saw one of us without the other. On Christmas, my freshman year of high school, he invited me over to his house, so of course I went. This day would forever change my life. We went up to his room, which was on the third floor – a small little space if I remember correctly, where he proceeded to caress me, kiss me and tell me how much he loved me. He was polite enough to ask me if I was ready and if I wanted to give it to him. "Why couldn't all guys be like this?" I thought to myself. I responded to him by helping him remove my clothes, and the rest, as they say, is history. This decision led to a whole new world of hurt and anger. When I arrived home, my mom's friend, who was like an aunt to me, said, "You had sex didn't you?" I just remember thinking, "How in the world could she know this?" I just gave her an awkward look and raced off to the bathroom to change my blood-stained underwear, and bathe. Apparently she had relayed this information to my mom, because the next day we were rushing off to the doctor for birth control. I must not have been taking it appropriately though, or either it was just too late, because a few months down the road I had a pregnancy scare and then a miscarriage scare. I missed a period and subsequently had a positive pregnancy test – at fourteen years old might I add. What the heck did I know about having a baby, especially as mentally messed up as I was? That was just not a good idea, on any level. One day I started bleeding pretty heavily, kind of like a normal period, so I headed to the doctor. I was told that I was probably having a miscarriage and should be on bed rest for a while, with my feet elevated. In hindsight, this was really funny! To this day, I believe that I must have just missed a period somehow and had a false positive test. Who really knows? Anyway, T, who was sixteen, was devastated. He really wanted to have this baby with me.

After this experience, I started to drift away from T a bit. I started to take notice of other boys, as they did me. There was one guy, in our new neighborhood, that started to stalk me somewhat. He would often be seen riding his bike back and forth outside of my home, and would follow me around. I had grown mildly afraid of him. One day I told T about this person when, yet again, the guy decided to case my house. Needless to say, off went T chasing him around the corner with a baseball bat. I honestly don't know what happened around the corner, but I do know that the guy never bothered me again. Unbeknownst to me at the time, this was a huge warning sign that T had become way too mentally attached to me. I recall another time that a guy I had been talking to on the phone, decided to pop up at my house while T was over. T answered the doorbell when it rang, and to his surprise, there was a guy asking for me. The guy left, and T decided to punch a hole through our living room wall. Warning sign number two!

Over time, T grew more and more obsessed with me, so engulfed in fact that when the time came for me to move on, he attempted to take his own life. And so goes another traumatic experience. I had actually started seeing another guy, while I was still involved with T.

My feelings for T were starting to fade, and there happened to be another young man persistently seeking my attention. One day T came over to my house, and I had this other guy's ring on. Of course he asked about it, and I, being the brutally honest person I was, told him who it belonged to. The next thing I remember is T running down the street pouring lighter fluid, which had been on our front porch, all over himself and trying to light his clothes with a lighter. Wow! Was this guy really this crazy? Furthermore, what idiot runs while trying to ignite a lighter? Obviously he hadn't thought that through. That moment was, in fact, the end of our relationship. I absolutely could not deal with this level of mental instability. I still had my own issues to deal with!

During the latter half of my ninth grade year I had to transfer to Shaw High School, where I experienced much more torment. Between fights, riots, drinking, and cutting school, I don't know how I made it out. I made lots of enemies, one of two ways: on the one hand, I was very intelligent. I had spent all of my previous years in "gifted" education programs, so naturally I expected to be in honors classes in high school. I was told, however, that they didn't operate that way. They didn't automatically put people into honors classes. See, at the catholic school I had transferred from, everything was considered an "honors" class, but since it didn't present that way on transcripts – well I guess they figured I was to fit in with everyone else. Problem was I never really did fit in anywhere. The other students started to become rather agitated with me, because I would either sleep through the entire class, or not attend classes at all, yet still manage to pull off an "A". It had gotten so bad that my mother was called up there and specifically told to make me act like I was paying attention because my classmates were complaining. To this day, I can't figure out why that was my problem. Anyway, the second source of my enemy stream came from the fact that guys found me attractive. Well this made the other young ladies quite upset. I even had the school's security guards wrapped around my finger. I would cut school, with the truancy officer, come back intoxicated, and sit and hang out with security until I sobered up enough to go back to class. One experience in particular, my sophomore year, will forever remain embedded in my mind. There was this girl who had been attempting to intimidate me for a while. She was jealous because her ex-boyfriend and I had begun dating. One day, I suppose she was feeling pretty froggy. She was a pretty popular girl, and she was able to enlist the assistance of about 30+ other girls to come after me one day. I believe that after a previous incident with another girl, someone must have told her not to approach me alone, I don't really know. Anyway, as I headed to lunch on this day, I was approached by this mob, and by then I had completely had enough! One of the school's teachers grabbed me and pulled me off to the office, and I could see this mob lurking outside the office. Of course, I had had enough backing down, so I grabbed the phone and called my home. My mom's best friend answered because my mom was at work. I said to her in these exact words, "If you don't come and get me now, you will be coming to visit me later in East Cleveland jail because I'm about to kill this bitch", and I hung up the phone. She must have felt the seriousness in my voice because it seems she was there in about 5 to 7 minutes. We were escorted out, and that was my last day at Shaw High. I ended up at Glenville High School, mid-tenth grade.

Right around age fifteen, my grandmother fell severely ill with cancer. We believe she knew long before we did, but I suppose we'll never really know.

My mom decided to become my grandmother's caregiver, after a failed attempt to hire someone from the outside. She stayed with my grandmother most of the day, every day, which pretty much left me free to do whatever I wanted. I had already been experimenting with marijuana and lots of alcohol, and although the marijuana use slowed down significantly, the alcohol use continued to increase. I had now added 32oz cups of liquor to my 7am walk to school. I was often too drunk to stay at school – a bad habit I picked up during my tenure at Shaw. Unfortunately, and yet again, I decided to take the "dummy" approach to my school life. A truly foolish decision in hindsight! My objective: to dumb myself down enough so that I would fit in, and not stick out like a sore thumb. This led me to hanging out with the wrong crowds, participating in gang activity (which, by the way, was initiated by my getting jumped by a group of girls – along with my newly found cousin by marriage – in the girls' bathroom at school), cutting school more, and drinking more. Funny, my mom was so busy caring for my grandmother, I don't believe she ever really noticed my downward spiral, until it was too late.

One day, while hanging out on one of the "hot" streets ("hot" because it was a notorious drug hot spot), I met a small time drug dealer named Erik. He and I began talking regularly on the phone, or would go grab a quick bite to eat or something. Nothing too major, until one day he asked me to run to his house with him to grab something he forgot. I, of course, thought nothing of it, and off I went. Nobody even knew that I had left the area. Once at his apartment, his actual motive reared its ugly head as I was being thrown onto his bed and asked repeatedly to remove my clothes. When I didn't comply, he decided he would simply take it. Now, mind you, at this time I had a very small frame, with the exception of having very large breasts. I stood about 5'8", but was only about 125 pounds or so. I fought with him as best I could, but ultimately, after having him violently pull my pubic hairs, I submitted. I just laid there with flashbacks of my childhood experiences, while he had his way. After he was done he sent me home in a taxi, and I never saw him again. I was so humiliated. I believe that I read somewhere that today, in the U.S., date rape accounts for almost 70% of sexual assaults reported by teenagers and college-aged young ladies. 70%! That's a ridiculously large number, and unfortunately is not as accurate as it could be because, like me, so many of us never report it. Just as before, this was my dark secret.

Around this time I had decided that sex would be MY weapon. I didn't want anyone to take it from me anymore. In my mind, it made perfect sense to simply do it, and turn it into somewhat of a game. This way, I remained in control. I had had enough of not having control over my own body. It was bad enough that I was a mess emotionally, while yet appearing so strong and in control.

A few months after this incident, I met another drug dealer through a girl I hung out with at school. I was often at her house, and he was a relative of hers. This was no small timer though; he had made quite a successful career out of selling drugs. He took an interest in me and never really gave me the option of turning him down. He was quite a bit older than me, but that didn't matter at all. Turns out, this guy, "Mark", would be very instrumental in my life over the next five plus years. Mark and I started to spend a large amount of time together. Unfortunately, he was also a womanizer, so

I was definitely not his only one. I was, however, the one he treated with the most respect. And he reminded me so much of my grandfather that I became pretty attached to him. He started to spend lots of money on me, entrusted me to hold large sums of cash for him, and paid me large sums of cash to allow him to use my kitchen to "brew" his concoctions, cook for him, give him sex, and pretty much anything else he requested. I knew that I was not his only girl, so I decided to venture out as well. Another acquaintance of mine introduced me to a guy who was about a year older than me. His name was Lance. He and I started having sex almost immediately, and ultimately became boyfriend and girlfriend. This continued on for months. That January, about a month after my sixteenth birthday, I got my driver's license. Naturally, being that he was my boyfriend, I ran to Lance with excitement. Later that day, once my mom left to go to my grandmother's house, Lance came over. We put on some music, "Secret Garden" to be exact, and engaged in sex right in the middle of the floor. Once finished, he rose up and looked me square in the eye and said, "Shay", which was my nickname at the time, "You're pregnant". I laughed at him and we talked for a while, then he left.

Now, and because I now had a driver's license, Mark would allow me to drive his cars. Mostly, of course, to chauffer him around. I didn't mind though because, again, he was paying very well. I also now got to drive my mom's car, so any time Mark called, I came running. If I couldn't get my mom's car, he would send for me via taxi or personal driver. It was all pretty cool to me at the time. Messing around with drug dealers did have a few drawbacks though, like dealing with their violent tendencies and their egos, just to name a few. Mark and I would fight sometimes. I remember trying to run him over with my mom's car once. He threw Chinese food all over her windshield, and for the life of me I could not get it off. There was no wiper fluid in the fluid tank, and I was stuck for a while having to get cups of water to clean the windshield enough for me to drive. Thankfully, my house was only around the corner from his. I also vividly recall walking home from school one day and literally being abducted by some guys in a minivan. I was so scared for that moment, until they got me into the van. Turns out it was Mark and his crew. I hadn't spoken to him in a while, and since he knew my schedule after having been stalking me for a while, he decided to take matters into his own hands. I didn't make it home from school that day until late evening. Funny how men think that sex and money can fix anything. I'll admit, at that age, it did sort of fix things. However, I did pull away from him slightly, and hung out more with Lance. A couple of months had gone by, and I hadn't had a period, but it was Friday so who had time to think about that? I got into a fight after school with a girl I had been going back and forth with for weeks, and proceeded to party and drink that entire weekend. Monday morning, however, I made my way to the doctor and didn't attend school. That day would forever change my life, again. I was, indeed, PREGNANT! "Oh my God – Lance was right", was all that I could say. People speculated that I wasn't in school because of the fight on Friday. They obviously didn't know me very well. I had a lot to think about on this day. Do I keep it? What will I do now? Will I be able to finish school? I mean I was only 16. What about partying, fighting, and drinking? Well I decided to keep the baby, and promised myself that I would not take another drink while I was pregnant. I went back to school the next day like nothing had ever happened. I did not share this news with anyone – after all, they would find out soon enough. The girl I had fought on Friday decided that, because she was with her crew, she would attempt another fight with me. I had to have the strength to ignore her. After all, I was going to be a mother. No one could figure out what was going on. They all assumed I was scared. There was only one person that I had confided in – that was my cousin, the one I had gotten jumped with in the bathroom. She was, indeed, the closest person to me. Later that day, I shared the news with Lance. His response was, "I already told you that". That is still creepy to me.

Around this same time, or shortly thereafter, early April in fact, I had gotten a message at school that my grandmother had passed away and I needed to come home. I was always the strong one in the family. I immediately went running to my cousin's class and grabbed her and off we went running up the street. My godmother met us at the house and drove us to my grandmother's home. Upstairs awaits an image that I will never forget. My Bunny lay peacefully in her bed, in what appeared to be a deep sleep. Unfortunately however, there was no more breath inside this now tiny frame. I broke down. I just remember feeling as though my legs were giving out beneath me. I grabbed the bathroom door frame for support and slid to the floor. This was, in fact, the worst day of my life. Here I am a couple of months pregnant and the love of my life is gone, and what's worse is that I hadn't really spent any time with her throughout her illness. She wouldn't even be around to fuss at me about being pregnant. My grandmother meant the world to me, and although I didn't show it often, I have never loved anyone as much as I did her. She died thinking I was just a bad kid with a horrible attitude, and not even knowing that I was pregnant. I wasn't a mean kid, I had problems...I needed help. Unfortunately for me, that wasn't how my family operated. I wish she had stuck around to see my growth and the changes that I would make within myself. I hope that you are at least somewhat proud of me now. I will always love and think of you.

I told Mark, about two months later, about my pregnancy. He, of course, thought the baby was his, and when I told him it wasn't, well let's just say he was not in agreement with me. He started to stalk me for a while, again, even sitting outside my house at 5:30 in the morning. I knew this because he would call and tell me to look out the window. He would always tell me that I would always belong to him. I suppose though that he eventually began to believe that the baby was not his, and pulled away a bit. We didn't really speak much until my daughter was a few months old.

During my pregnancy, the father and I fought a few times. I recall when I was about 7 months pregnant, one of his friends tried to talk to me. When I shot him down he got upset and went and told Lance that I had come on to him. For some reason, Lance believed him over me, and upon confronting me, slapped me so hard that his handprint was left on my face until the next day. I always carried a pocketknife, so I took it out, but he snatched it and broke it against the brick wall of the school we were standing behind. I was pretty much done with him at this point and after that incident we only spoke on occasion. I had met another guy in school, who seemed to really like me, and so we started to date.

One day, he was over to my house and we were sitting on the porch when Lance drove by with some of his friends. Needless to say, he backed up and came storming onto my porch and tried bullying me into the house and trying to intimidate the guy. Neither attempt worked so he jumped back into the car and sped off. Soon after that, we moved again and Lance and I had not spoken again until the day Alyssa was born. I remember this night as if it were just last night. I had been on bed rest for a couple of months and unable to attend school. I was up late because I was uncomfortable and couldn't sleep. I finally laid down around 1:30 in the morning, and by 2:00 I was right back up in pain. I had never had a baby before, so this feeling was not familiar to me at all. I thought I had to go to the bathroom, so I went and sat on the toilet, but nothing came out except a ball of mucous that was tinged pink. It was time. The house we lived in was rather large, and my mother stayed on the third floor with her own phone line. I called her and when she answered all I could say was "mommy help". She came flying down the stairs and called the ambulance. My contractions had started off being 5 minutes apart, and by the time the ambulance got there they were three minutes apart. I really believe that the father of my child had some sort of sixth sense or something because he showed up ringing my doorbell at 2:10 in the morning, at the exact moment that I sat down on the stairs to wait for the ambulance. I don't even remember telling him where I lived! He said that something just told him to come over. He did go to the hospital with us and watched her birth, all the while fussing at the doctors for checking my cervix for dilation.....MEN.

My experience at the hospital was anything but pleasant. First, the monitor kept malfunctioning, my contractions were now two minutes apart, and the nurses were very rude. When I finally got on the table, I had dilated five centimeters and holding. The doctor was on the phone with the anesthesiologist, just outside of the room, trying to order an epidural for me when I felt the baby's head coming out. I yelled to the doctor…screaming in sheer terror, "I feel the head coming out!" "No you don't", he told me, "you're only at five centimeters, and I just checked you five minutes ago". At this point my mom went over to the door and politely threatened him to come check me again. Within 10 seconds the room was full of people. Her head was, in fact, coming out. I had dilated from five to ten centimeters in five minutes! Lance stood there and cried as I gave birth to our child. It was really cute to see him in tears.

My daughter, my beautiful little angel, had to spend the next nine days in the NICU (Neonatal Intensive Care Unit), due to the ingestion of meconium. She was a week late and thus had her first bowel movement in the womb where she ingested it and it stuck, like tar, in her lungs. My precious child lay there with tubes and wires coming out of and connected to everywhere on her little 7lb 14oz body. This was now the most traumatic time in my life. I stayed by her side the entire time, especially because there was one red-headed nurse there who I caught, on several occasions, speaking very badly to the sick infants. She would say things like "I wish you would just go ahead and die already". It was so disturbing, and with my violent past, I really wanted to hit her, but didn't want to go to jail and leave my baby. As luck would have it, someone turned her in as I watched her being arrested on the news a few months later.

Lance and I continued to see each other for about six weeks or so, but that was it. He had met someone else, and eventually had a child with her as well. He has since had a child with another young lady also. What's still funny to me is that, with that kind of connection, one wonders why he never really played a part in the life of my daughter. Oh well, his loss.

Over the course of the next year not much went on, except that I did receive a full-ride academic scholarship to a private, Catholic college in South Euclid, OH, called Notre Dame. I, of course, was too stupid to accept it, and thus, turned it down. Out of all of the things that I have been through, not accepting this opportunity is the one I regret the most. I also experienced the loss of one of my dear friends. I had gotten back into the streets a bit, and had started seeing Mark again, as well as a few other men. I was also going to night school to catch up so that I could graduate on time. I used to catch a ride to night school from my "big brother", or so I called him. He was a close friend of Lance's. Because they were in the streets, they had a rival group of guys who they would often fight with. One night, this group came onto Lance's turf and began shooting and sped off. I happened to pull up shortly thereafter to find my "big brother" lying dead in the middle of the street with a bullet hole through his eye and out the back of his head. I saw fragments of his brain and skull in the street. I lost it! I tried to hold him and talk to him, as I screamed and cried. The guys took off looking for the perpetrators. I am still upset that the ambulance wouldn't allow me to ride with him to the hospital. I knew he was gone, but I still wanted to hold on. This was horrible. What's worse is that he was actually the good one out of the bunch. He didn't want to fight or get into any trouble with the other guys. I loved him dearly. I will always miss you, Lamont.

At this point, I didn't really want a man to get too close to me emotionally, so my interactions were only about sex. It was as if I couldn't stop. For some reason, I felt afraid to stop. Men were nothing to me, but at the same time I had some subconscious fear about saying no. So instead of saying no, I used them for sex and money, and for that time, I was content with that. I stayed with T for about a year or so when I was 14, but after that, and up through today, I have never really been successful at having a relationship. After all, I had never actually seen a functional relationship. Even my grandmother's marriage was based on security. Her husband was an alcoholic, but he managed to hold down a really good paying, secure job, and although she didn't really seem to love him, she stayed with him because he was a good provider. They didn't even sleep in the same bedroom...ever! He was rather creepy to me anyway.

In trying to cope with all of my emotions, and fill some void that was left from not having a "real" father, I probably ended up with hundreds of men during my teen years, and didn't start to regret it until my late twenties. At that time, it was all some kind of sick and twisted fun. I still thank God daily that I have not, to date, been diagnosed with HIV or AIDS.

In the early part of 1992, Lance's crew had thrown a house party. I was already back in party mode so I couldn't wait to go, even though we were not together. I had actually been seeing another young man. He was really cool, and really into me, but to me, it was just sex - part of the "fun". He was definitely not getting my heart! At this party, I was the door checker. I would pat everyone down as they entered because we didn't want anything jumpin' off. Apparently I, unknowingly, got pricked in the finger with something that night because, for the next two days, my middle finger on my left hand was swelling out of control. There was also a visible red line travelling up my arm. The party was on a Friday night. On Monday morning I decided to go to the emergency room because I was unable to stop the swelling. After cutting off my ring, and running some tests, I was admitted to the hospital where I subsequently spent the next five days, on an antibiotic drip. The doctor told me that I had blood poisoning and that was what we could see travelling up my arm. When I went in, the red line was about three quarters the way up my upper arm, and the doctor said had I waited one more day to come in, I would not have survived. He said that had the poison reached my heart, there would not have been anything that they would have been able to do for me. How could I be this near death and not even realize it? I was so frightened. What if their drugs wouldn't work in my system? I had just had a baby, I wasn't ready to go. Thankfully all turned out well, except that the infection seemed to reoccur for the next few years, sending me off to the emergency room each time.

Around October of 1992, I met a man who was just getting out of jail, at his release party. This guy swept me off my feet. At the same time he was asking someone about me, I was asking about him, and we were connected from that point forward. I was even recently supposed to marry him, but we will re-visit that ridiculous story later. All I knew was that I had to have this guy. It was just something about him that made my legs weak. Funny thing is that he wasn't even really that cute to me, but he had some kind of magnetic attraction that would not let me go. "Johnny" was his name. Everything was great for a while. He was a thug and loved trouble...and I hung on to every bit of it. All I knew was that I was Johnny's girl, and everyone in the hood knew it too. Guys were even scared to talk to me now because of him. This was fun! I fell so deeply in love with him that I would have probably done anything to please him. Oftentimes I would have to go pick him up in the middle of the night after a shootout or fight or something, take him to steal a car, or some other crazy escapade. I didn't mind any of it, I was

Johnny's girl and that was all that mattered to me. Johnny introduced me to a girl who would become my best friend. She was pregnant when I met her, and her boyfriend, at the time, was Johnny's best friend – and a real piece of work.

A couple of months into our relationship, I ended up pregnant. I was so excited to be having Johnny's baby! All of a sudden however, things began to go downhill. He was disappearing more frequently and not calling me as much. One night I even picked him up from what I later learned to be another girl's house that he had been messing around with. I was so fed up at this point that I too ended up meeting someone else, who told me that he could not be with someone who was pregnant by someone else. This person would later prove to be almost fatal. His name was "Terry", and we will discuss him in further detail in the next chapter. I was just about four months pregnant, fed up with my so-called boyfriend, and wanting to pursue another guy. So what would my irrational thinking self do? You guessed it! I went to the abortion clinic. It took a two day procedure, but I killed the child growing inside of me. I know many of you hate me now, but it's ok, I hated myself for long time because of this decision. It wasn't until 2011 and finding Jesus, that I finally forgave myself. Johnny knew nothing about my contemplations and subsequent proceedings of having an abortion. He didn't find out until about a week later when he decided to call me to ask how his baby was doing. I, ever so smart-mouthed replied to him, "What baby? You don't have any more babies over here". He was pretty devastated, and so I stayed out of his path for a very, very long time. In the meantime, I hooked up with Terry, who ironically, I had had a crush on many years earlier as a young child. I was now 18. We'll continue this saga in chapter 4.

Push Through:

My teenage years were a mess. Most of which I wish I could go back and change. They were completely filled with tragedy and drama, with the exception of the birth of my baby, which was immediately followed by drama and trauma. I experimented with sex – no matter the person's sex - drugs, violence, and alcohol, any of which could have cost me my life. Sorrowful that I can't go back and change the things I did and the decisions I made, I just continue to ask God for His forgiveness and mercy, and try to push on, because it is only through Him that I find strength.

I would just like to tell any of you that may be going through some of the same things, to get help. It is vital to your emotional, physical, and spiritual well-being. Do not simply believe that you can handle all things on your own as I thought I could. There is always at least one person who will listen, even when it feels like no one understands. For you, *I* will listen. Do not allow life's circumstances to overpower you. As hard as it may sound, you have to remain in control, and by that I mean knowing when to seek help. Do not allow negativity to consume you, because it can and will faster than you can even imagine. Keep your mind filled with positive thoughts and surround yourself with positive people all the time. Even if it means letting go of someone you care about. God will replace them with someone who truly cares for you.

Understand the power and importance of family. Although we cannot choose who God puts us with, we can choose to love them and to continuously be a part of their lives and make them a part of ours. Life is so very short. You may not have another opportunity to tell someone that you love them. I was devastated that my grandmother left me and that I had chosen the streets over spending her last days with her. This is something that I will never be able to change. All that I can do now is hold on to the soothing thought that I will one day see her face again.

Young ladies, please do not diminish your self-worth by choosing to use sex as a weapon or a tool of any sort. Your body is your temple – you only get one. Don't allow your temple to be destroyed by evil. Evil comes in many forms, trust me, because I believe that I have come face to face with all of them. I do not want any of you to live even a percentage of the life that I did, nor do I want to see you make any of the destructive decisions that I made. Trust yourself and the Lord, He will never steer you wrong. Remember that He loves you unconditionally, and is the only one that can. He will forgive you of anything that you have ever done, if you just seek Him and ask. Also know that you must also forgive yourself, this is the very first step in recovering the person inside of you. Without forgiving and loving yourself you will never be able to forgive or love anyone else. I am here to tell you that unforgiveness and bitterness are not paths you want to choose. Forgiveness is the ultimate feeling of release and freedom. While you are making yourself sick, with anger and resentment growing rapidly inside of you, the person who offended you is most likely sleeping soundly at night. Believe that you have a greater power on your team and that love truly does conquer all.

The Sound of Fear Chapter 4

For the first few weeks Terry was great. We talked on the phone all of the time, and he kept a smile on my face. I suppose it's true what they say about a person sending their representative to meet you until they get you roped in. One day, we were sitting in front of his parents' home, in my mom's car, when I happened to turn my head to the left because I noticed a figure out of the corner of my eye. There was a young boy, probably around age 15, walking down the street. Terry accused me of staring at this guy and flipped out! He grabbed the keys out of the ignition and threw them across the street into the grass of the vacant school which, by the way, was nearly up to my waist. Then he spit in my face all while yelling obscenities at me, and telling me to go find my keys. I really wanted to fire back at him and tell him to go find the keys, but honestly, at this point, I was kind of scared. Being scared was an emotion that I hadn't felt in quite some time, so I wasn't really sure how to process this. Terry had been drinking that day, but, at this point, I was still unable to put two and two together.

See, Terry was a violent alcoholic, but it wasn't until incidents kept happening, that I actually realized this. One night we were sitting on a side street, near to his home, in my mom's car. She had a blue Oldsmobile...I remember it well. What I don't remember is what made the demon rear its ugly head on this night. I do recall ending up locked inside the car with him and the keys on the outside! He kept hollering at me to get out of the car, but I knew if I did something awful would happen to me. He picked up the largest stone he could and threatened to bust me out of the car if I didn't get out willingly. Apparently I didn't move fast enough for him because the next thing I heard was the sound of this huge stone crashing into the hood of the car. "Oh my God! What the hell am I supposed to tell my mother?" This was all I could think of to say as I jumped out of the car. I don't believe I ever told her the truth about this incident. I remember making up some story about some kids throwing stones off of a bridge at cars or something like that. I'm sure she knew better...I wasn't a really good liar. I remember seeing flashing lights up the street, and thinking if I could only make it up to them, maybe they would help me.

So off I went running. Now this guy was an amateur boxer, so he was pretty in shape. Me, on the other hand, well I was just too cute to think about physical stuff. Of course, he caught me. He started hitting me so hard that I fell to the ground, where he began kicking and stomping me. I just remember laying there crying. I don't even know how I got home.

Ahhh, now that I think about it, I believe that fight started because I said hello to one of his friends that had gotten into the car with us. I was not allowed to speak to any male. I forgot this rule once again and got my mouth busted open. I stayed away from my mom for a while until my mouth healed. I really didn't feel like trying to come up with another story anyway.

One time we were over to one of his friends' house, whose girlfriend and I had actually become pretty cool, where once again, I became the punching bag. His friend liked me. I could tell by the way he always looked at me. On this particular day, I was in the bathroom looking in the mirror, and when I looked up the friend was standing there. He leaned in to kiss me, but I backed away. I did not tell Terry, and I don't know how he found out, but when he did, of course it was all my fault. This sounds like déjà vu. I guess he was more upset that I didn't tell him. He beat me up in the back of their apartment building. Every time, so far, he had been drinking.

We were sitting, one day, on one of the busiest streets in Cleveland, Euclid Ave. We were parked in front of a barber shop where he was to get a haircut. My oldest daughter and I, who was two at the time, were hanging out in the car. Out of nowhere, he came out and snatched her out of the front seat and threw her into the back seat, through the car window. I got scared so I hurried and locked the doors, but had forgotten to roll up the car windows. Anyway, I was going to do whatever it took to protect my child. He was trying to reach in and grab the keys from the ignition – thankfully I had left the car running. I started rolling up the windows on his arm while he kept trying to punch me. I was parallel parked in a tiny space, so with my free hand I was trying my best to maneuver out of that spot, while fighting him off, and after hitting the cars behind and in front of me several times, I managed to get out. His arm was still stuck in the window as I took off down the street, but he eventually got his arm out and I kept going. I was terrified and shaking like a leaf. I got as far away as I thought I could safely, then pulled over to check on my daughter. She was visibly shaken up, but seemed not to understand what was going on. This was so unfair to her.

He suckered me back in after that fiasco, and I thought this next incident would be my turning point. If only I had been so lucky. One beautiful afternoon, myself, Terry, and my daughter – still two – were all sitting on the front porch of his home when Johnny (remember him from earlier) and his best friend, who was staying up the street with his other girlfriend, rode by. They hollered, "Shay, what are you doing down here?" Remember, they hadn't seen me since I had gotten the abortion. Now they didn't stop for a response or anything, they just kept on driving. Not realizing, I'm sure, what that innocent question was about to unleash. I was holding my daughter in my lap, stupidly thinking that he wouldn't do anything if I was holding her. He kept asking me who that was, and I told him it was some old friends. I suppose that answer wasn't good enough for him because before I had a chance to blink, he hit me so hard in my right eye, that I literally saw stars. He barely missed my baby girl. The entire right side of my face was huge, and black and blue for weeks. That same night, he chose to stay with me at my mother's house, on the third floor. I had moved up there since having the baby. This is the night that I knew, beyond a shadow of a doubt, that God truly did exist. I had already been sleeping with a rather larger butcher knife tucked away by my bed, and that night, it almost got some action. Terry was sound asleep and before I even thought hard about it, the knife was at his throat. Something shined on me at that very moment – maybe it was just the moon – but I heard a voice that said softly, "don't do it", and that was all. Tears started streaming down my face and I was shaking like crazy, but that presence made me put the knife down. He was never aware that he almost died that night.

After that incident, I went back to an Air Force recruiter that I had been speaking with about my options to get away from all of this. I had sunglasses on, but I guess he could still see the bruising underneath. "He did this to you?" "Yes" I replied, with my head hung low. He reached over and lifted my head and began kissing me. I swear, I must have "take me" written across my forehead! He got up, locked the door and closed the blinds, and led me to the back of his office where he proceeded to take my clothes off, while kissing me ever so gently. My emotions were so mixed up right now. This guy was military, with a family, and was supposed to be helping me, and yet something in me wanted it, even needed it. He got inside of me and expressed interest in killing Terry for me. However, he opted to get me out in the next batch of recruits headed to basic training. I later learned that he put in for a reassignment out of state. I guess he didn't want his secret to come out. Within about a week or two, I was off to Lackland Air Force Base in San Antonio, TX. The problem with this whole situation was that I didn't really want to go. I was just running away. So, as I am sure you have already speculated, I was back home in about two and a half weeks – which is probably why that recruiter hightailed it out of Cleveland. My next move would be the single most stupid thing I've ever done and it nearly cost me my life.

When I returned from basic training, I ended up seeing Terry and was back with him again. This time however, I guess he and his family had devised a plan to keep me for good, and not allow me to escape. They all got together, and somehow without saying a word, threatened me with regard to staying with him. We ended up at the Justice of the Peace, married. "Oh wow, seriously?" This was all I could think of. I was hoping that somehow the Justice of the Peace would see the terror in my eyes and rescue me. That didn't happen. I knew that had I said a word, or tried to get out of marrying him, he would kill me. I went home that day and just handed my mother the marriage certificate. She was so upset with me that she didn't speak to me for quite some time. If she had only known what I was really going through, however this seemed to be the norm, she never knew what I went through. Truth is, I didn't really want her to have to deal with the truth anyway. So, fearing the worst and hoping for the best, I was now the 18 year old bride of a monster that I both feared and hated. August of 1993, we were married, and I had been made to live on the other side of his parents' duplex with no utilities, or food. I wasn't allowed to go out and get a job for fear of me running away. My daughter stayed with my mom. Thank God! So there I stayed, in this awful house, with only a couch, and having to occasionally go next door into his parents' home for a shower. As you can imagine, I lost a lot of weight, not that I had any to lose because I was already very small. We ate a lot of "penitentiary" food – mostly mixing different things from a can together. God, how I hated this man! He would force me to eat this stuff, and then force me to have sex with him by holding me in wrestling moves. I was so sick from the stress.

There was an old lady that lived around the corner from my mother's house. I don't know how Terry knew her, but we were at her house a lot. This was also a disgusting experience. Her house was so dark and nasty. There were rodents and roaches everywhere. It was horrible! We fought quite a bit in front of her house as well, mostly because I wanted to go to my mother's house, instead of this woman's house. By this point, I was so afraid of him that every time he would even raise his voice, I would vomit. Luckily, sometimes my throwing up would stop him from hitting me, at least for a while anyway. He started to believe that I was doing it on purpose, but I wasn't. I just couldn't help it. Even if I was at my mom's house and he called, I would vomit.

Now you would think that this went on for years, God knows it felt like it. However, it was actually only a couple of months after we were married. One night, it had to be in October, I was at the duplex and he came in drunk, as usual. This night however, seemed a bit different. Something just didn't feel quite right to me. He began threatening my life, and saying that if I ever tried to leave or talk to anyone he would kill me. If I had never believed anything he ever said before, I believed him this night. Now normally when he came in drunk, he would attack me for a bit and then pass out. This time, however, by someone's watchful eye, he left back out, saying that he would "take care of me" when he got back. I peeked through the window coverings to see which way he went, and waited about 5 minutes or so, then I took off running around the corner! This was a neighborhood where I was, in essence, being held hostage so I knew absolutely no one. I started frantically knocking on doors, thinking that any minute he would catch me. Thankfully, there was an angel behind the second door I knocked on. There was an older lady who answered, and I was shaking and in tears, and I told her that I was running away from my abusive husband, and asked if she could please just let me use her phone. She agreed. I called my friend Tracy, I loved her so much, she was always there for me, even letting me stay with her for a short time after Terry blacked my eye once. She immediately came to pick me up. I didn't know what time of the night it was, but I was surely grateful for the two of them that night. If only the drama had truly ended there.

Terry started stalking me, daily, at my mother's house. He stayed around the corner a lot, either at the bar or at that old lady's house. He would call my mother's house constantly, threatening my life. He would leave dead roses at the door regularly. All I could think was that this was the type of stuff you only saw on TV. I was very afraid to leave the house for a long time. Thank God, he eventually stopped for a while, and during this lull, I regained my self-confidence, and eventually was no longer afraid of him and, in fact, dared him to come anywhere near me. By this point, I had vowed to kill him if he ever touched me again. It was also during this time that I enrolled in school for Medical Assisting, which I started right away, and by February, had filed for divorce. The divorce went uncontested and was granted in August of 1994. To this day, I don't know why I never called the police on him. Fear I suppose, I really don't know.

Just to test my new-found level of confidence, I actually went to him once when he called. I met him over his aunt's house, who just happened to be a very interesting lesbian. I don't judge anyone's lifestyle, because Lord knows I have done lots of experimenting myself. She was just an interesting person. That's all I'll say about her. Anyway, I went up to that apartment, just as cocky as I could, and stood in the bathroom doorway to see what he had to say. He wanted to know why I left him and why I filed for divorce. "Are you for real?" I snapped back. He tried to get tough and come at me, but I pulled my blade and stuck it right up against his throat, and said with a smirk, "I wish you would, please give me a reason". He backed off...quickly. It made me think that if I had just stood up for myself a long time ago, perhaps none of this would have happened. After all, he wasn't any bigger than me. I believe I let the fact that he was a boxer and a former high school wrestler, intimidate me.

Later that same year, I started dating a stripper. We were out at a club one night, along with my really good friend that I had met in medical assisting school, and guess who I bumped into on the dance floor. Exactly! Terry! By this time, I was back to my healthy weight, and looking fabulous again, when he decided to pull me aside to talk. I just laughed, but feeling tougher than I had in the past, I obliged. I had my switchblade close at hand. I was wearing a sexy, black bodysuit underneath a gold, zip-up sweater – which, of course, I had unzipped. He reached over and tried to zip up my sweater so I smacked his hand away and told him not to touch me. I think we were both shocked. He said something about the divorce, but I proceeded to walk away, and that was the end of the conversation, and the very last time I have ever seen or heard from him.

Push Through:

Ladies, I can only ask you to please not allow yourselves to go through what I went through. You simply don't have to. Now, I understand that everyone's situation is a little different, and some may have kids involved, no family support, no friends, and other such issues, but there is ALWAYS a way out. Please don't allow him to break you down so far that you believe him when he tells you that no one cares and that no one will help you. I know how much easier said than done this is, but I did it and so can you. I would simply say to make sure you have an exit strategy in place first. I did not, but thankfully I had a mother who loved me no matter what. To you beautiful teenage girls living this nightmare, you have entirely too much living to do. This does not have to be the end for you. *He* is not the end for you. Do not give him that power over you. Please do not believe that you can change him. I am telling you from experience that it does not work that way. Do not be afraid to get law enforcement involved. At least while they have him in custody, you can make an escape, even if you have to leave the state. Do not ever compromise your life, or the lives of your children, because you love this man.

Don't go blindly forward believing that things will get better someday, because there may not be a someday for you to make it to. God did not put us here for this. Understand and accept that we make mistakes sometimes, especially mistakes with who we choose to be with, and it is ok to walk away, especially when it was not who God intended for us. The person God has for you would never even dream of treating you this way. Trust me when I tell you that anyone who could hurt you like this DOES NOT love you! I do, however, because we are connected by this bond of pain, and so does God. You are His child, remember that. He does not smile upon someone hurting one of His children, and His desire is for you to be safe and living abundantly. It is Satan that wants you to succumb to your fears and weaknesses, don't allow it, because he has already been defeated according to the Word of God.

Ladies, just don't give up or give in, the world needs you in it, healthy and strong. Please remember that you are beautiful, intelligent, and strong, and there is absolutely no reason for you to EVER let anyone other than God control your life!

A New Beginning Chapter 5

After ridding my life of Terry, I found myself evolving into a new being, or so I thought. Right around the time I had signed up for school, I had also begun a job at a very ritzy downtown hotel, in the housekeeping department. I was 19 years old by this time, and after working there for a few months, I went out and bought myself a new car. During my tenure at the hotel, I met lots of celebrities, mostly basketball players, but I also met a really great guy. He was beginning his career in the record industry, and was working street promotions, travelling around the country for a very notorious record label. He and I began spending lots of time together, as he

would often make his way back to Ohio for "work",
although he lived in L.A. I am thankful to say that he
and I are still good friends to this day. He treated me
like royalty whenever he came around. He would buy
me clothes, give me money, get me into all the clubs,
and have me backstage at all the concerts. It was
quite fun and made me love the person that he was.
Even when they were partying with all the "hoodrats"
that would come around because the celebrities were
around, he would kick them out when I was on my
way. He seemed to respect me, and I was in love with
that. One night in particular, he and his crew were
apparently having some kind of wild party in the
hotel room when I called. He told me they had a
bunch of strippers there and were just having fun, so
I politely let him know that I was on my way, and
before I even hung up the phone, I could hear him
clearing everybody out. I got to that hotel as fast as I

possibly could but unfortunately, as I handed over my keys to valet, I was detained by a then up and coming rapper trying to hit on me. I, however, was on a mission so I wasn't really giving him the time of day and turned his advances down.

This was during the winter time in Cleveland. He got so upset with me for brushing him off that he started throwing snowballs at me as I was trying to get into the hotel. "What the hell!" Was he serious? I mean first of all, I was way too cute for him to be throwing frozen water at me! Some years later this particular rapper ended up spending quite some time in prison for charges of rape against some other female. Obviously he wasn't very good at handling rejection. I swear...men are something else! But, I guess I wasn't too much better because later into our "relationship", I found out that my record industry friend was actually married, and had been for quite some time. Supposedly he and his wife had an "arrangement". I'm not really sure what that meant and I never really asked any further questions. All I knew was that when he was around, my friends and I were living the high-life!

Around this time I also moved into my first home. It was in the 'hood, but I thought I was tough so it was all good. My friend from school had introduced me to this guy, who she called "Party Man". I fell completely head over heels for this guy, and even let move into my place for a while. Unfortunately he cheated on me the whole time with his ex-girlfriend. Therefore, he had to go. I credit him heavily as well for my distrust in people. I must say though that I had started back seeing Mark anyway, so I guess I shouldn't have been as mad as I was. Oh well. Mark was married by this time, and had another girlfriend, both of whom had found out the truth about our relationship. They had originally been under the impression that we were just friends and that I sort of just "worked" for him. Either way, I really didn't care. He kept enough money passing through my hands that none of that even mattered. Mark and I were pretty inseparable. Even when we fought or went a while without speaking to each other, we always managed to find our way back to one another. He would always say to me, "Shay, all you have to do is have my baby and you will be set. You wouldn't have to worry about anything". The one time I was possibly pregnant by him (although it could have been by a guy I met just entering the fire academy), I had an abortion. I mean, I got whatever I wanted anyway, why did I have to have his child?

It is amazing to me how I survived going to school and remaining on the Dean's List this entire time. After all, I was usually up all night smoking marijuana and/or drinking, working, and occasionally dodging bullets. My best friend's brothers had quite a few enemies, all of whom seemed to be able to spot our cars wherever we were. It had gotten so bad that I told my mother she would have to keep my daughter for a while because it was just not safe for her to be around me. I am so grateful for my mother's support of my daughter.

Johnny came back around this time as well. We were still friends and would be there for each other if we needed. He was always there to protect me when I called him, and hung around with us quite often as well. He did, however, have a girlfriend now. One that I knew was a lesbian, but he was obviously too naïve to see that. Anyway, one night he came over to my house and we had the most passionate sexual experience I believe we've ever had. Then, he returned home to his girlfriend. I was pissed! I raced over there, jumped out, and started slashing his car tires. I was so mad and so jealous! How dare he come make love to me like this and then go home to her? There was just no way he was getting off this easily. A few minutes after I returned home, still fuming, Johnny pulled up. He had gotten a ride from his best friend. He burst into my house and slapped me so hard that I had to regain my composure, but once I did all I could do was laugh. I don't even know why I was laughing. He called me a "crazy bitch" and left back out of the house.

After a while, I had lost my job at the hotel because I ran out one day to go to my best friend's aid whose boyfriend had beat her up. The same guy that had brought Johnny to my house the night I slashed his tires. She called me at work crying and I could think of nothing else but getting to her. I tried to come back to work the next day, but I guess they had a different idea. So between getting fired and people popping up at my house at all hours of the night, I ended up moving out of my house and back in with my mom for a short while. It was during this time that I learned of my alleged biological father. I say alleged because it would later be proven that this was not the case. It started with me meeting his aunt. I would go and care for her and spend time with her because she was aging with failing health. One day an envelope of money came up missing, or so she says, and she accused me of stealing it. It took everything in me not to curse her out. "Are you serious lady? I don't need to steal from you. I am not now, nor have I ever been a thief." Yes I have been many things, but stealing from someone, especially family, was not my persona. That hurt me so deeply that I never spoke to her again. I did, however, use a phone number that she had given me, to initiate contact with the man that I believed had helped give me life. This was disastrous! When I told him who I was, he responded by saying that I was not his, that my mother had been raped by a group of guys, and that if I wanted a DNA test I would have to pay for it. Mind you I was in Cleveland, OH and he was in Berkeley, CA. How was I to manage that? I couldn't afford a blood test, let alone one that would span across the country. I simply hung up and cried....hard. It would be a significant amount of years before I would speak to him again. This was so hard for me. I was devastated. I wanted so badly to get to know him, and to meet any sisters and brothers I may have. My world was destroyed at this point. The whole in my heart was quite large, and growing. I could feel my strength diminishing yet again.

Around this time, I had graduated from school as a Medical Assistant, and although this was certainly beneath my potential, it was a rewarding accomplishment. I truly regretted not accepting that scholarship after high school. My life did begin to change for the better however, as I began my new career. Although I still drank and partied heavily, I was just as focused on my career. I even spent some time in Florida caring for the mother of my medical assistant instructor.

In the summer of 1996, my friend from the record industry came out to see me. By now he had been moving up in his career and was more of an executive I believe. He took me to a concert, where for some reason he left me, and I ended up stranded there. I walked across the street to a bar and sat down for a drink. Up next to me comes a guy asking me about the peanuts in the bowl in front of me. I was so not in the mood for this right now, but he was persistent, and sweet. I ended up telling him that I had gotten left there and didn't have a way home, so he made sure I got home that night. He and I talked a lot on the way to my house, and continued our relationship from there. One day, I remember him asking me how many men I had slept with, and I told him about 10. Ha! Our whole relationship was now based on a lie. I wonder if I had actually told him the truth...that it was probably more men then I could count, would we have continued on. He had just gotten out of prison the day before we met, unfortunately, drugs were his lifestyle. Not using them, but distributing them. The lie that I told him ate at me every day. I really didn't like lying.

Anyway, our relationship continued on and we spent most of our time together, including one night in October that I was supposed to be going to my friend's birthday party. He was dead set against it though and wanted me to be with him instead. So I accommodated him, and we spent the night in his brother's basement. A couple of months later, I found out that I was pregnant. By this time, however, we were not on the best of terms. His "career" had picked back up, and he was out of town most of the time. I was jealous because he had been spending most of his time with me, and now that time was gone. Now I was pregnant however, and felt kind of stuck. I told him about the pregnancy, and he, to my amazement, was super excited. I thought about getting another abortion, but I had already had three, and he threatened my life should I even think about it any further. He swore that when the baby was born things would be different, but in the meantime he had to do what was necessary to "set things up". Whatever! I wasn't buying any of that crap. Especially since, during the times he was there, his pager would go off all night. Once, I responded and it was a female on the other end. I was livid and had no problems letting him know that. He, of course, got pissed at me for answering his pager. He told me that I messed up his "place" out of town, that he supposedly worked out of. Again, whatever! We got over that though, and he was there when my second daughter was born. We even ended up moving into a home together, and for a short while things were ok. I had since had two very impactful deaths, Tupac Shakur, who I admired and loved dearly, and my aunt. My aunt and I were pregnant at the same time when I was carrying my first child. She was 40 and I was 16, she was a heroin addict and I was wild and reckless, so we both had a problem with the other being pregnant. Our daughters were born two days apart, and now they were about to turn 6. I had gotten custody of her daughter after her death who, unfortunately, was born addicted to heroin. She would have screaming and crying fits where she would literally tear her own hair out. This was very difficult for me to deal with during this time in my life so I ended up walking away from everything. I signed my cousin over to her paternal grandmother. I wanted to do the right thing so that she wouldn't end up in foster care like her older sister, but I was drained, just completely drained. Then one day while my daughter's father was at work, I cleared out the house and moved into an apartment. I just couldn't take any of it anymore. Plus I had built up such a strong resentment toward my daughter's father that once the endearment that I felt watching him hold her when she was born wore off, I was completely over it all. He accused me of being selfish, and maybe in hindsight I was. In my defense however, I was working a lot of really crazy hours, trying to care for these kids, worrying that my sister's father, who was a drug addict at the time, would sell my kids while I had him babysitting for us while we worked, not having time to cook for everyone, getting up at 5:00 am to make his coffee, giving him sex, trying to lose the baby weight, and on and on... Ugh! I'm getting upset and exhausted even just thinking about it again. It was over for me. I had never really had an actual relationship, and I was not domestic at all. I hated cooking and cleaning! I didn't know the first thing about keeping a man happy. My attitude was still horrendous, and as far as I was concerned it was my way or no way. Sometimes, I do wish I had stayed with him and tried to find a way to make it work. Overall, he was a good man and a really good father.

I was so depressed for a while after I had moved out. There was so much going on in my world, and my daughter's father had met someone else and was now living with her. One night, the kids were gone and I had a horrendous headache. I had been getting migraines since around age 15. Part of me just wanted to sleep and never wake up. I took about 15 Tylenol that night, and a tall glass of vodka. I think I called my daughter's father to say goodbye, and he called 911. I remember waking up in the hospital. Gratefully, I was fine. I am still thankful for him because, through the years, he has continued to be there for me, even after he ended up marrying the girl he was with, which by the way, I was devastated about. Funny how everyone managed to keep that a secret from me. I had since moved to Atlanta, and the kids were with my mom, in Cleveland, for the summer. They all attended the wedding. My daughter was even the flower girl! What the heck? How does this happen? How does my whole family attend this wedding and I know nothing about it? I guess it shouldn't surprise me since obviously my family was really good at keeping secrets. I took it all very personal, I think they believed that I would have driven up there and acted a complete fool had I known. They may have been right. I guess we'll never know.

The ATL, wow! This was most certainly all that it was cracked up to be. Although, I must warn you against renting an apartment sight unseen. There were so many fine black men there that I felt almost overwhelmed. I, of course, attracted only the crazy ones. Some were stalkers, who couldn't take no for an answer, others were just overbearing and would try to do anything to get and keep my attention. I got into quite a few night club spats for guys touching me after being told nicely not to, while others got to take me home, or sometimes just out to the car. One, in particular, stands out above all the rest. His name was Mike.

Mike and I met over a summer that the kids were in Ohio. I would get really bored without them and go down to the bar to shoot pool. I picked up a few skills watching the guys play and having them show me how to play. This guy was there one night and he and I couldn't seem to take our eyes off of each other. We flirted a lot, and ended up exchanging phone numbers. Instantly we seemed to be connected at the hip. So much so that he eventually moved into my home. I bought him a car, and helped him get a job, and after that, I was sick of him. This seemed to be how I operated. I couldn't tolerate people for too long. I don't understand what kept allowing me to move people in with me. My mother says I've always been like that. I've been moving people in since I was a child. She's always seemed to be pretty accepting of that. She says that I like to take care of people and to try to fix people. Maybe it was because no one ever tried to fix me, I don't know. In either case, I was getting pretty fed up with Mike. It seemed that everything he did annoyed me, and everything he didn't do annoyed me even more. I started being very nasty toward him, and trying to get him to leave but he wouldn't. What was I going to do? Run away you say? You got it! That's exactly what I did.

All the way back to Ohio. My excuse was that I was going to go to nursing school full time and needed to be back home with the support of my family for the sake of the kids. So just as quickly as I packed up and headed there, I packed up and headed back. Leaving a great job behind I might add.

On a side note, this job taught me a lot about teamwork and loyalty. It was during my stent at this job that we experienced the terror attacks of 2001. This was a blood banking job, and although we worked almost 48 hours straight through that time, we learned how our country could come together, and what it took to be there for each other. I really liked that job and hated to leave it, but I had to get away. Unfortunately however, this was not the end of my experience with Mike. He decided that he would follow me there. I guess I should have been clearer about the fact that I did not want him. I just assumed that my moving out of the state, without him in tow, would be obvious enough.

After I was all settled in, he shows up at my door. I had given him the address so that he could write to me if he wanted to. Stupid, stupid! I let him in, but I was ruthless. I would leave and not come back all day, every day. I would talk to him any kind of way. One day I guess he got fed up, and while I was over my best friend's house, he smashed all the glass in my house and wrote "Bitch" in my Bible. He called me to tell me he had done this and that he would be waiting on me when I got back. Apparently he didn't realize that I was home now so he had no chances up here. My best friend rode back with me, and on the way we called Johnny. When we got to my street, my best friend drained all of the air out of his tires, and we sat outside until Johnny and a carload full of his young minions, pulled up. He instructed us to stay outside until they cleared the house. They went rushing through my house like SWAT. Mike was nowhere to be found. He must have realized that it was war. You don't come up here destroying people's property. I never saw him again, and the car was gone the next day. Johnny stayed with me that night. It was nice, and felt just like old times.

He and I continued to see each other for a while, mostly, I believe, just so that he could use my car and come and sleep somewhere he felt comfortable. I ended up pregnant yet again by him, although I don't think he was too happy about it. I learned that he still hadn't really forgiven me for having that abortion several years before. I guess I couldn't blame him. I had a really cushy job at the time, and had started nursing school. Unfortunately, I ended up having a miscarriage, and while I was devastated, I suppose it just wasn't meant to be. After the miscarriage, Johnny and I had stopped seeing each other and didn't really speak much at all anymore. I took on a second job at a local hospital and ended up meeting another guy there. He seemed kind of shy, although flirty, so I had to be the aggressor. I gave him my number and we began dating. This was around April of 2003, and around this same time my great grandmother passed away. My mother had been caring for her for quite some time. Mind you I had only been back in Ohio since the previous August.

In June, I had a tummy tuck and around this same time my mother called and asked me if I wanted to move to Las Vegas with her. She said that since my great grandmother had passed away, she was sick of the cold in Cleveland, and wanted to now spend time closer to her brother who lived in California, but had a few properties in Las Vegas. "Of course I will" I replied. After all, my lease was almost up, I hated the cold, and I really didn't have much, other than school, going on in Ohio. When I got back to work however, after the surgery, things got a little more serious with this guy that I had met at the hospital, who we'll call Jason. He asked me to marry him one night while I was taking a bath. For some reason, I agreed. Why, I don't know. I didn't love him or anything, but he was cute and we had fun together. Plus, I felt like I wanted to be married. Who even knew what that really meant? I hadn't seen any successful marriages. Thus again, another man moved in with me. I let him convince me that he should just move in now since I obviously couldn't move to Las Vegas without him, and we could save some time and money by just moving everything from one house. To this day I don't know where he came from or who he was living with prior. I would later learn that nothing he ever said was true. My lease was up in August, and off we went to Las Vegas. Funny, the day we were leaving was the day that almost the entire northeast and mid-west part of the country went black with some kind of freakish power outage. It was August 13, 2003 I believe. I should have taken that as a sign. I am so stubborn that it is just ridiculous!

Push Through:

Emotions are dangerous! It is not wise to allow them to rule your actions and reactions. This is how so many people end up killing senselessly, in jail, or emotionally destroyed and disturbed. I believe I fit into the latter category, but could have very easily fallen into one of the others. I am very thankful that I have been protected through all of my emotional outbursts. God has continued to watch over me, even though I wasn't acknowledging Him appropriately during these stages in my life. I need for you ladies to understand that living life so guarded, emotionally charged, and not trusting of people is a destructive combination. I understand that you may have been hurt. I get it like no one else, but what I need for you to get is that forgiveness is the key. First, you must forgive yourself as we discussed earlier, and then move on to the people who have wronged you. I am just mastering this and it is a daily struggle, but it is the absolute most rewarding feeling in the world. Use your emotional energy to forgive. Attitude is also another key factor. The attitude that you choose to have when attempting to handle tough situations may make all the difference in your coming out victorious or not coming out at all. I say choose because we are the only ones who can control our attitudes. No matter the actions of others, we can choose how to move forward. Understand that people are just that...people, and we cannot expect them to be perfect in any way. We cannot even expect them to do things as we would. It is simply not fair. You will continue to be hurt if you continue to have such high expectations of people. I know that you say that all you're asking for is respect, or honesty, or whatever it may be, but I'll be real with you...stop expecting it. Put that type of expectation in God because He is the only perfect one, and the only one that can truly change any of us.

This chapter was called A NEW BEGINNING, but as you can see, nothing really changed. I wasn't ready yet. I wouldn't be ready for quite a few more years. I continued to find myself back in situations of abuse and destructive behavior because they were familiar to me, and even though they were extremely unhealthy, I just didn't feel as if I deserved any better. You will know when you reach your breaking point. This will be the point when you either roll over and die, or find the greatest weapon there is and fight. Without God as my arsenal, death was the only

other option.

Vegas Baby! Chapter 6

Being that the power outage decided to happen on the day we were leaving Cleveland, I got a pretty sweet deal on a U-Haul truck, because they had no way of accessing my electronically scheduled pick up. The guy said, "Just give me $150.00 and take the truck". Cool, I thought, this would save me a little bit of money. Never count your blessings too early, let me just tell you. This truck was a nightmare! It refused to travel over 40 mph, and somewhere along the way it spewed oil out of the engine and all underneath the hood. It took us five days to reach Las Vegas. It was the most painstaking trip ever! Especially since I had to drive the entire way. Why, you ask? Well because this guy, this one I was to marry, tried to flip us over when he was given the opportunity to get behind the wheel. He would most certainly not get that chance again. Along the way, in Illinois somewhere, I had to take myself to the hospital for chest pains. I thought I was having a heart attack. Turns out, it was an anxiety attack. Why oh why did I not pick up on all of these signs? Anyway, we finally arrived safely in Vegas, where I had never felt that kind of heat. It was the middle of August and about 113 degrees. Jason and I unloaded the truck into our little apartment, and were ok with each other for a short while, but pretty soon my attitude started to flair, and my patience and tolerance levels were near empty. Sometime before November, he ended up moving with a friend he had met, and dating some other girl, who by the way, was supposed to have been pregnant by him. Worked for me, I really didn't care too much anyway. Somehow he ended up back at my place though, really wanting to work things out, he said. Fine, whatever. The whole marriage thing started being tossed around again, and around income tax time that next year, I found myself paying for a wedding, and everything that went along with it. I even got ridiculous tattoos for the both of us with each other's names. When I tell you I didn't make very good decisions, I mean it....seriously! As I was taking that walk down the aisle, that February, at that little white wedding chapel, the only thing that kept coming to mind was, "turn around and walk out the door. Hell, you paid for it anyway". Instead, I kept walking forward, feeling more nauseous with each step. It's funny how our bodies warn us when we're about to do something really stupid. I guess you either listen or you don't. If this wasn't confirmation enough, how about taking a look at the wedding night? We went and partied with some friends at a night club, then stayed at a hotel on the strip, on my dime of course. What does he do when we walk in the room? He passed straight out from drinking so much. So I spent my wedding night alone in the Jacuzzi. One night was all I could take so we went back home. There the fun really started. He figured that since we were married now, he owned me, and yes he even had the audacity to say that out loud. My mission became to prove to him that he was nuts for thinking something so ridiculous.

From time to time, however, we got along ok. We hung out on the strip and other local casinos gambling a lot. I even helped him land a great job with the county, through one of my patients at the lab where I worked. It was a good position with quite a few potential raises, and that was working out pretty good for a while. Around this time I had gotten a fully-loaded Lexus LS 430, with TVs throughout. It was black with black leather interior, 20in rims, the works. I had gotten the car from a friend I met at another lab I worked at. She was going through some domestic abuse situations with her then boyfriend, and could no longer afford the note on the car. I took over the note for her. He was so jealous he couldn't stand it. He would go flashing in my car like it was his, cruising on the strip with all the TVs on like he was balling. What a joke!

One night, we were on our way home from hanging out somewhere and began arguing about something stupid, the car I believe. By now it was late July, and the kids were in Ohio for the summer. He swung over at me in the passenger's seat, so being that I had gone through this enough before, I swung back. We began exchanging blows in the car until we reached the apartment. I jumped out and started to walk away, but he wanted to be Mr. tough guy and come after me, so we fought some more in the parking lot until the little old lady downstairs from us came outside. Everyone thought he was a sweetheart. He was very good at manipulating people into believing that. Shoot, he got me like that too! She stayed out there talking to him, and I went upstairs and got in the bed. When he came in, he said, "I'm going to be moving out so you don't have to worry about me anymore". "Great", I responded, "how soon?" The argument ensued from there and before I knew it he was on top of me trying to choke the life out of me. He just kept repeating, "I will kill you, I will kill you". I remember feeling my eyes close and when I woke up there was urine in the bed where I was laying, and he was now on the side of the bed, still yelling. I wasn't really coherent so I'm not real sure what he was saying. I was now faced, yet again, with the decision of either killing him in his sleep, or calling the police. There was absolutely no way I was letting this crap slide again. After he fell asleep, I called my daughter's father to ask him what he thought I should do. His response was this, "You know I don't condone bringing the law into your business". Was he saying I should just kill this guy then? I paced around the kitchen for a while with the largest butcher knife I could find in my hand, but all I could think about was my girls losing their mother to incarceration. I wasn't sure enough that I could get off on self-defense. This was a new state with very different laws so I didn't want to chance it. I put the knife away and lay back in the bed. The next morning, after he left for work, I decided to call the police. Before I realized it my apartment had become a taped off crime zone. It was like some stuff you see in the movies. They were taking pictures of my neck, took my bed sheets, took my house phone, and went to pick Jason up at work. He was carted off in handcuffs so I heard, and subsequently lost his job. He spent the next 35 days or so in jail. During this time, I moved out, and into one of my uncle's places, and tried to start over. It was hard though because there was so much communication from the attorneys and detectives. He went in on a bail of $300,000, but later conned the judge too, who reduced his bail to only $1.00. He still got stuck with a felony assault record though, which still follows him to this day. I'm not really sure how he was savvy enough to make people believe this innocent facade he put up, but not smart enough to get himself out of a felony. Dude, you had the judge in the palm of your hand. What happened? I felt sorry for him when he got out, and ended up allowing him to move back in with me in late 2004.

I had never gone through with the divorce that I filed while he was locked up so we were still, in fact, married. Things were actually pretty decent for a little while. Once again I helped him to get a job at the place I was now working. Thankfully they didn't have background checks. I would find myself often having to put some chick in her place for flirting with him. No one actually knew upfront, except the people that hired him on, that we were married. Pretty soon however, everyone knew. That didn't stop some of them from trying though. I suppose it's true what they say about karma, because I had had my share of other people's husbands. My mom had finally moved down to Vegas by now – it took her a whole year after I had already come here. She and Jason had both started to almost beg me to have another child, and although I wasn't really overly agreeable, I decided to give it a go. I had stopped taking my birth control shots, and one day in the early summer of 2005, decide to sleep with Jason to see if I would get pregnant. I had been counting the days from my period, so this was the time of ovulation. Lo and behold, it worked! About 6-8 weeks later I tested myself at work and I was surely pregnant. I could already tell though because my attitude was ever increasing. When the result popped up on the test, I called my mom immediately. While sitting there talking to her, one of the lab techs came over and decided to give me grief about being on the phone. I just remember looking over at her and saying, "Bitch, if you don't back away from me, I'm going to punch you in your mouth". I suppose threatening people at work causes a hostile environment or something because the next day, when my boss found out, I was fired. So I just sat at home, pregnant, collecting unemployment until around October when we moved into a house. The landlord of this house was a real estate agent who offered me a job working as his assistant. I accepted the job and worked for him for a while, and in the meantime got my Realtors license. I worked right up until the day I went into labor. My son was born super bowl weekend, 10 lbs. and 1oz. He was beautiful with a head full of hair. So beautiful and big, in fact, that the nurses took off with him, and I didn't see him until later that day.

The whole marriage thing just wasn't working for me. While I was pregnant and after I had the baby, I would stay at the office from early morning until late at night. I just didn't want to come home. It was only because of the kids that I did come home. It was so bad that I didn't even wait six weeks after having the baby to go back to work. I used a couple of weeks to study for the Realtor exam at home, and then went and took the test and was right back at work. Around February of 2007, we moved again, and this is where the stuff really hit the fan. My daughters could not stand Jason. I mean he wasn't very bright, and that just didn't sit well in my household. He couldn't keep a job or a car, it was just ridiculous. One day we started arguing again, and he had gotten pretty loud and tried to snatch my son away from me. My girls were there this time though and called the police when they saw him reach for me. The police came out but no one was arrested this time. Apparently he had already met some chick because he ended up moving in with her. He would always call me wanting to come back so I decided to play with them both, because he had since admitted to having her at my house while I was working, and they were there with our son. I played along with him; even going so far as to tell her that there was no way she could win against me. He would always come back if I called. I made him come over one night, and had sex with him. Of course he was back the next day. "I told you girl, don't mess with me, I'm a beast!" was what I told her one day on the phone after that. I tried to hang in there for a little while, I mean after all I could have just left him where he was.

During this time, my mom and I decided to take a trip to California to meet face to face with the man who was allegedly my biological father. I was living pretty decently, working in the medical field, and by now they sold DNA tests at the local pharmacy. Once there, we met his family, and I felt so very connected to them. I felt that you could see the resemblance in our faces and mannerisms. It seemed that everything would blend together perfectly! He and I drove off together and talked. He apologized for the way he had previously treated me, and I, of course, forgave him. We swabbed our mouths and sent the test kits in to the lab, and thus I was headed back to Las Vegas. During the waiting period I was so overjoyed and anxious. I believe I must have called that lab 50 times. Turns out though that the lab lost his kit! I was furious! They offered to send him a new one, which they did, and the test was subsequently performed. The results were negative. This man was **not** my father. I was devastated...again. So devastated, in fact, that I all but accused him of not performing the test appropriately on purpose. I tried to ensure him that I wanted nothing from him. I simply wanted to have a relationship with my siblings. He has since upheld his claim to have completed the testing accurately. Oh well...

My relationship with Jason didn't last very long this time around, and he had convinced the girl that he had moved in with before to let him back in. I used to talk about the fact that she was just a big girl with low self-esteem, but in hindsight, I was obviously not too far off from that myself. Later on that year, close to Christmas, he emerged again, begging me to take him back. He couldn't deal with her size anymore, and she was getting on his nerves. So, maybe it was the Christmas spirit, but I went and got him. When I pulled up, they had already been arguing and fighting I guess, because she had bleached all of his clothes and personal belongings, and had thrown them all outside. I was in my truck trying hard not to laugh. I was still so immature. I blocked her in the parking space of her apartment and dared her to get out or say anything, but she took the high road and found a way to maneuver out. I laugh at myself now.

For a while he and I were good. This was our rollercoaster. Not long after however, I just couldn't continue to keep up the charade. I told him that he could continue staying in my home for a short while to save me the cost of childcare, but soon enough even that wasn't working out for me. So I did my usual and started looking for a place to move to. This was late summer of 2008. Shortly before I was ready to move, I told him to go. I am not sure where he went, but I was sure he would find some chick to let him in. I moved mid-August, and filed for a divorce early that following year. It was granted early 2010, with no contesting, and with full custody of my son. I kept his last name because my son had it, and because I had since started a phlebotomy training company, and it would have just been too much extra work to change everything back to my maiden name. After moving on, my ways hadn't changed too much, with the exception that I was heavier in weight, so my self-esteem had dropped significantly. It didn't affect me as much on the East coast and in the South because, although smaller than I now was, the guys seemed to like the weight. On the West coast however, I wasn't getting as much attention. I still managed to sleep with a few different guys, one I even kind of liked. We were getting pretty close pretty fast, but then he backed off. Scared I suppose. We are still friends, but I was pretty annoyed with him for backing off. Oh well, again I say, whatever!

I was starting to try to figure out how to change though. I started reading all kinds of self-help books, and praying. I mean I really wanted to change. I didn't want to have the same attitude, the same opinions, and the same reactions. I wanted to learn how to make friends, love someone, be loved, heck be liked for that matter. I started really focusing on the inner me. I got shaken up a little around April of 2011. I prayed really hard one night asking God to send me "the one". I was so tired of feeling lonely, and not ever having anything real. The next morning, when I awoke, I had a message on Facebook from Johnny. Where had he been all of these years? He was just getting out of prison, again. Weird huh? I took this as a sign. He immediately started wooing me from afar. Telling me how he always knew I was the one, and that he wanted to marry me when he was completely free. He was living in a halfway house in Cleveland. This went on for months, and everything he wanted or needed, I did or got, including a cell phone. Our agreement was that I would pay for it until he was released since the halfway house was keeping his checks from his job, and then he would pay me back. I still can't stop laughing at how stupid and blind I was. Anyway, it was really fun for a while. We would have lots of phone sex, and would talk through the night. It was amazing. That was until the cell phone bills started coming. Who did these numbers belong to that he would stay on with for hours? Me, being the insecure person I was, decided to call the one that came up the most. Just as I suspected, it belonged to some girl from the neighborhood. Apparently he was also making promises to her, and sexing her when he could get outside. He was supposed to be on the bus to work, but instead he would have her pick him up and use that extra time to get some. Wow, still a jerk! We fell out a bit about that, but I gave in after a while, especially since I was almost 3,000 miles away and couldn't do much about it. So I, of course, reverted back to what I knew best. I sought attention elsewhere. I went to have a massage at one the well-known massage chains, and the guy giving me the massage began innocently flirting. I decided to kick it up a notch! I mean I was naked and he was a man, a white man at that.

I suppose my flirting turned him on a bit too, because he decided to step out to see if he had anyone waiting behind me. When he returned he said we were free for a while, and asked me where I wanted him to massage next. My response, "anywhere you want", so I felt his hand starting up my inner thigh, eventually landing on and inside my vagina. I was still mad at Johnny and this was sweet revenge to me. He played with me for about 15 minutes then I thanked him, tipped him, and went home. As twisted as it was, it made me feel better.

Johnny swore that he would be here as soon as he was out. As time went on however, our conversations became less and less frequent, and I was noticing all of these Facebook messages back and forth with another girl, who by the way, he was old enough to be the father of, *and* who was also just released from prison and staying in the same halfway house. I had all of his passwords to everything because I was the one that set everything up for him. These messages between the two of them were getting very steamy and more and more frequent, so I decided to confront him. Of course he was quite pissed that I had been snooping, but I didn't care. I felt like he had played with my emotions and I was heated and ready to go on a rampage. Instead, however, we began parting ways, and I decided to pray more and attend church. For a short while I got involved with an adult group that discussed sex day in and day out, and it was during this time that I had a breakthrough. I had hit a new low in my life and one Sunday morning, as I set out to a church across town that I had visited a few times, I remembered seeing a Facebook post about another church. I put the name of it into my GPS and ended up driving there instead. As I stood there listening to the choir sing, I cried so hard that I didn't think I would be able to stop. When the pastor began to speak, it was as if there was no one else in that sanctuary but me and him. I believed that he was speaking directly to me with every word he uttered. I gave my life to Christ on that day, and that was the best decision that I have ever made...literally. I was so tired. I had to slow down. Sex was my strength and my weakness. It "fixed" things for me, or so I thought. Even though I wasn't engaged in it as much as I had previously been, I jumped at most chances I got. White, black, male, female, – it didn't really matter to me. This had to stop. Thank you, God, for continuing to love me despite my obvious and intense dislike for myself.

Push Through:

From the moment I gave my life to Christ I could see everything a bit clearer. I can look back at my past and understand the mistakes that I made all along the way, even up until the very moment I walked up to that altar. Now I am not saying that I haven't slipped up along this journey, I have...more than once. What I can say is that I have been blessed with forgiveness. I have been able to forgive myself, and all who I believed had wronged me, including the man who molested me for years and my mother. I had also all along been blessed with the power of discernment, I was just choosing not to listen to it. I am not saying that I don't still struggle with my attitude, my sexual appetite, my insecurities, jealousy, and anger, I do. However, I now have a stronger presence fighting with me, one that I have openly accepted and who loves me unconditionally. That is a feeling unlike any other, just to know that you don't have to fight alone.

This entire book has been very therapeutic for me, but it is meant to help at least one person deal with some challenge they may be facing. It is not meant to demean anyone, male bash, or expose anyone's business but my own. I just really wanted to reach out to women and young girls in the hopes of preserving their self-worth, self-confidence, self-esteem and self-love. Never let go of your soul and your fire and passion for life. We will all face many obstacles during our stay here on earth, there is not too much we can do about that, but believe that there is a higher power that will see you through any storm, as long as you have faith. There were many times in my life that I could have and wanted to just give up, but I didn't. No matter how hard things have gotten, and sometimes still do, I understand now that this too shall pass, and that the strength of the Lord is all that I need. I am begging you to stay strong, reach out to people, read the Bible, do whatever it takes for your survival. There is always a way to push through the pain, no matter how dim the light seems at the end of your tunnel.

I'd like to leave you with a couple of scriptures that helped me along the way, even before I was saved and baptized. This is just to reassure you of God's love for you:

Proverbs 3:5-7: "Trust in the Lord with all thine heart; lean not unto your own understanding. In all thy ways acknowledge Him, and He shall direct thy paths. Be not wise in thine own eyes; fear the Lord, and depart from evil."

Isaiah 40:29-31: "He giveth power to the faint; and to them that have no might, He increaseth strength. Even the youths shall faint and be weary, and the young men shall utterly fall; but they that wait upon the Lord shall renew their strength; they shall mount up with wings as eagles; they shall run, and not be weary; and they shall walk, and not faint."

These scriptures are especially powerful to me because I felt as though I needed to always be in control...I had to know the reason for everything. They helped me to understand that sometimes we may never know the explanation for some trial we're faced with. All we really need to know is that God knows best. Just like I found myself on this journey in hopes of helping you, you may find yourself on a mission as well where you can then look back upon your life and say, now this is why it was all worth it.

I Love You.

Father...Unknown

So many sleepless nights

So many tears.....for so many years

Wondering about my birthright

...My father...

The one who contributed to...

The creation you have before you

But why bother?

I mean I guess somewhere in my soul

I just really needed to know...

Do I look like you?

Walk or move the way you do?

My sassy attitude or ever-changing mood,

Did those come from you too?

It's hard to feel so out of place,

Lost in a world with only half a face

I mean, obviously yes, my face is whole...

But not knowing you was like

Someone drilled a hole to the very core of my soul

And I was left

With only half a breath

I know...you say come to grips with reality

But I say....No!

I'm coming to grips with eternity,

'cause I found a new life and all has been forgiven

Christ saved my soul and carried me, broken, to my
real father

Up in Heaven.

Check out my interactive Internet Radio Show
entitled,

Never Strong Enough

This show will engage women in their quest for
strength, love, self-worth, confidence, and joy. We
will support and lift each other along the way.

You can follow and interact with the show at

www.blogtalkradio.com/never-strong-enough

Additionally you can find me at:

http://www.sourayachristine.com

http://www.twitter.com/sourayachristin

http://www.facebook.com/sourayachristine

www.ingramcontent.com/pod-product-compliance
Lightning Source LLC
Chambersburg PA
CBHW051827040426
42447CB00006B/403